THE AGWU DEITY IN IGBO RELIGION

A Study of the Patron Spirit of Divination
and Medicine in an African Society

By

Jude C.U. Aguwa

Fourth Dimension Publishing Co., Ltd.

First Published 2002 by
FOURTH DIMENSION PUBLISHING CO., LTD.
16 Fifth Ave, City Layout, P.M.B. 01164, Enugu, Nigeria
email: fdpbooks@aol.com, nwankwov@infoweb.abs.net
Web site: http://www.fdpbooks.com.

ISBN 978-156-399 0

CONDITIONS OF SALE

Design and Typesetting by
Fourth Dimension Publishers, Enugu

Contents

Foreword

No full study of Igbo religion has been made, and available accounts of even the formal subjects of beliefs and cults are incomplete. This statement made by G. I. Jones four decades ago about the studies of Igbo Traditional religion remains largely true even today. However, since he made this statement, a number of insightful works have been published on Igbo Traditional Religion especially in the seventies and eighties. Notable among these are Arinze's monograph, *Sacrifice in Ibo Religion* (1971); Ikenga-Metuh's *God and Man in African Religion: A Case Study of Igbo Religion* (1981), Professor Nwoga's *The Supreme God as Stranger in Igbo Religious Thought* (1984), and Ezekwugo's *Chi: The True God in Igbo Religion* (1987).

Thus, with the exception of Arinze's work, this generation of studies of Igbo Traditional Religion, focussed almost exclusively on the concept of God and Igbo world-view. The next generation of publications show a shift from concept of God to Rites and Rituals. There are, for example, Ikenga-Metuh's *African Religion in Western Conceptual Schemes: The Problem of Interpretation,* Ejizu's *Ọfọ: An Igbo Religious Symbol,* Ekwunife's *Consecration in Igbo Religion* and Nwahagh's recent Doctoral Thesis: *Kola Nut: An Igbo Religious and Social Symbol.*

The present work by Jude Aguwa marks yet another shift of focus in the studies of Igbo religion. The book: *The Agwụ Deity in Igbo Religion,* is the first of its kind on one of the many important deities of Igbo religion. Although belief in God is the undergirding belief of Igbo religion, the central focus of the rituals, festivals, symbols and morality in Igbo religion are in fact the deities, not the Supreme Being . Hence the study of the phenomenon of the belief and worship of the deities is really the study of the central core of Igbo Traditional Religion. If this affirmation is true, then the study of the essential elements of Igbo religion has just begun with the publication of this work. It is however, the first of many studies waiting to be done on this theme. For, the other important deities of Igbo religion like *ala*

(Earth Deity), *amadiọha* (Thunder Deity), *njọkụ* (Yam Deity) *ikenga* (Fortune Deity), are yet to be studied. Dr. Aguwa's study of the *agwụ* deity in Igbo religion opens up to us the riches and complexities of the world of Igbo deities, of which *agwụ* is one of the most enigmatic. For example, *agwụ* is reputed to be the most intelligent of deities, and yet is known to be the Spirit of recklessness and confusion. He is at once the bestower of healing power, and a wrecker of mental health. He both harasses and blesses his devotees.

The book is a product of an extensive and thorough research which took the writer to different Igbo cultural zones. His research method is a combination of personal interviews and observer-participant methods. His approach is a phenomenological and comparative approach. Themes covered range from beliefs about *agwụ* deity through the rites and initiation into the *agwụ* cult to the guild of diviners and traditional healers. The book is well written, and will be a very useful book to, not only anthropologists and religious scientists, but also those in the medical and pharmaceutical sciences.

Professor E. Ikenga-Metuh,
University of Jos.

Preface

Agwụ, the Igbo patron deity of health and divination is a well known phenomenon. Especially in the past, the evidence of the wide diffusion of belief in this deity in Igboland was very visible. There were shrines to it located at most family homesteads. Its symbols were always to be found at the shrines of other deities. Most communities had some persons who were *'agwụ* people', victims of its malignant powers, or recipients of its positive influences such as the priest-diviners and physicians. These features exist in the present times although sometimes in lesser degrees. Others persist in modified forms as a result of pressures of change, a sign also of the resilient nature of the indigenous religion.

Agwụ has an intriguing nature. As deity, postulate or hypothesis it is a fascinating and evasive paradox. Human experiences that baffle logic are easily explained with *agwụ*. Take for instance the situation that between the *dibia* who cures diseases and the mentally sick person *(onye ara agwụ)*, is the issue of *agwụ* as bestower of healing power and as wrecker of mental health. Is *agwụ* superstition, religion or reality?

What the major issue is, in a research on such a well-known subject is not the availability of information. It is rather, sifting the abundant oral information to obtain reliable data for a presentation of a pan-Igbo view on *agwụ*. This is why the phenomenological and comparative approaches in this work are so pertinent. It is expected that this work will serve the cause of the on-going discussions on religion, culture and humanization in Igboland and Africa.

Okuku agwụ (ọgwụ), the ritual calabash on the cover page is a highly polymetaphoric object of *agwụ*. First of all, it calls to mind the mythical basket, in which at the beginning *Chukwu* (God) had hidden the secrets he wanted the deities to name. Only *agwụ* could name them. *Chukwu* rewarded *agwụ* for his intelligence. *Agwụ* is the *ọkọnkọ* (one who guesses correctly),

vii

the wise one. *Okuku agwu*, the primordial basket of divine knowledge has begotten the ritual basket of *agwu* cult where the *dibia* houses the symbols of his *agwu*. This basket is revered as a dwelling place of *agwu*. *Okuku agwu* is the *dibia's* calabash of power. He stores his medicine in it and its power is measured according to whether it has one eye (hole) or more. When *Ezedibia* (chief medicine-man) shakes his *okuku* of many eyes, then powers are provoked. That is the time they sing of the *dibia:* to shake hands with the *dibia*, is to shake hands with the masquerade, and to shake hands with death.

At every stage in this work some people made important contributions. First of all I would like to express my gratitude to Rev. Dr. C. Ejizu, of the University of Port Harcourt for his helpful encouragements and expert advice. The Centre for Igbó Studies during her seminar series provided the forum where, from time to time, my research findings were examined. I am grateful to the entire staff of the Centre, to the participants at the seminars, and especially to the former director, Professor G. N. Uzoigwe and the present one, Dr. U. D. Anyanwu. My deep gratitude goes to Dr. Afam Ebeogu, Ichie P.A. Ezikeojiaku, Sr. Dr. Eberechukwu Anosike, Dr. J.O.J. Nwachukwu-Agbada and Okechukwu Okoro for their commitment to the manuscript. I appreciate the assistance of the following during the field research trips: Father Vincent Umekwe at Nri, Father Gody Odibo who introduced me in Igbariam, Fathers Peter and Bob at Illah; Father Joseph Nnadozie at Aku; Father Christopher Anyanwu Azuka at Enugu-Ezike; Mr. Ibiam Arunsi of Abia State University who accompanied me to Edda and Mr. George Ukaonu, my guide in Obioma Ngwa. I thank Mr. Okey Nwosu immensely for his involvement in this project. There are several other people whose contributions are important whose names are not mentioned because of lack of space. I am indebted to them all.

Jude C.U.Aguwa

SUBCULTURAL ZONES OF IGBOLAND

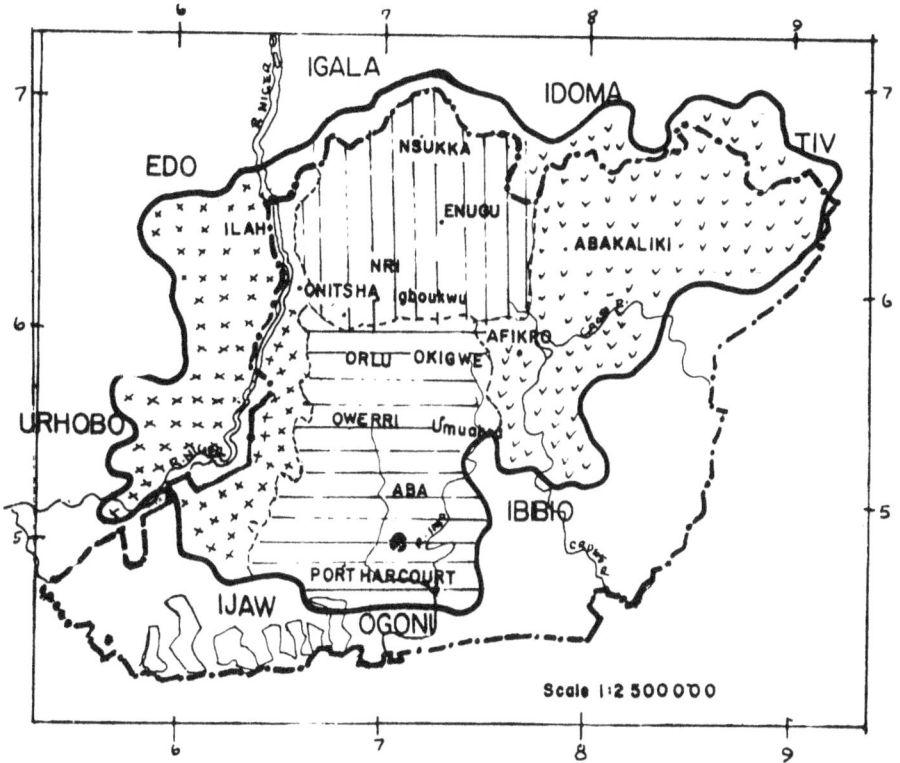

Scale 1:2 500 000

KEY

‖‖‖	Northern Igbo
⊞	Southern Igbo
∨∨	Eastern Igbo
✗✗	Western Igbo

Introduction

Agwụ is a household word in traditional Igbo society. It is the deity that patronizes the medicine-man *(dibịa)*. It is also believed that it afflicts those who refuse to become its devotees by possessing them, in order to punish them. Consequently *agwụ* is one of the basic Igbo theological concepts employed to explain good and evil, health and sickness, wealth and poverty, fortune and misfortune. Since most people, at one time or the other have the need of the institutions of health that are superintended by *agwụ*, belief in it is highly diffused. Rather than being considered an abstract or an otiose deity, it is perceived as being very close to the human world, as human-centred, and as part and parcel of human daily experiences.

The cult of *agwụ* is quite elaborate in the Igbo religious tradition and there are devotees of varied grades. Its power manifests in the lives of people - children, men, women - as 'negative or positive experiences. The negative effects of *agwụ* are found among those whom it afflicts with physical, mental, social and economic disabilities and woes. But there are also specialists such as diviners, physicians and priests who are possessed by it, and who acquire the expertise to harness its positive divine powers.

The powers of *agwụ* are recognized not only by human beings but also in the spirit world. This belief is embodied in some religious myths and stories as well as expressed in rituals. A mythical account from Itu Ezinihite in Mbaise, explains how *Chukwu* (the supreme God) assigned to *agwụ* the function of sharer and divider among the deities and spirits and as a result, in the family shrines, *agwụ* is hardly found absent:

> *Chukwuabiama* called all the deities one by one and asked them to describe the objects which he had hidden in a closed basket. Every one of them failed. At last *agwụ* was called and when 'she' came, she told *Chukwuabiama* the contents of the container. *Chukwuabiama* declared her the sharer and divider among the gods and thereby handed every

1

power to *agwụ*. That is why *agwụ* is to be seen in every family shrine or collection of deities.[1]

Ritual expressions indicate clearly that *agwụ* is not only a personal spirit of human beings but also of the other deities. Hence there are *agwụ chi (agwụ* allotted to a person by the supreme being), *agwụ ụwa (agwụ* of reincarnation), and there are also, *agwụ ala (agwụ* of the earth goddess), *agwụ amadịọha (agwụ* of the god of thunder and lightning), etc.

Agwụ is unlike the other deities of the Igbo traditional religion for it is constitutively attributed with contradictory qualities. It embodies negative and positive influences for which it is said to be ambivalent and capricious. *Agwụ* is both a destructive and a creative force. It may be compared to *Esu* of Yoruba religion or to the deity, *Legba*, of the Ewe and the Fon religions. People worship *Esu* and expect to be rewarded with protection from their enemies and to win other benevolences. But on the other hand, *Esu* is reputed to be highly mischievous and to be a wrecker of fortunes. *Legba* likewise is noted to be as beneficent as it is maleficent. This study hopes to provide elucidations on the nature of *agwụ* and of the ability of human specialists to obtain, use and manipulate its power.

We shall articulate the abundant data relating to this subject in six chapters. The first chapter will make a cursory survey of Igbo ideas of the supernatural world and disease causation. This is intended to present the Igbo cosmology and its dominant religious element. The consequence of such a religious world-view is that human conditions are taken to be ordained by gods. The Igbo believe that in relation to health, human biological, biopsychological, and parapsychological conditions are determined by deities, especially *agwụ*.

Chapter Two takes up the question of the human-centredness of *agwụ*, and considers some hypotheses of its origin, the modes by which its power and effects are transmitted

---

1   Interview given by Nwogu Ugorji, a diviner, and reported in Donatus Ibe Nwoga, *The Supreme God As Stranger In Igbo Religious Thought*, Hawk Press, Ekwereazu (Imo State, Nigeria), 1984, p.45.

from one individual to another, as well as its effects which manifest in many spheres of human life and activities. It draws attention to social structures and beliefs to which the deity is adjusted and through which its transmission is explained.

In the Third Chapter varieties of *agwụ* symbols are examined. These symbols are artistic, natural, phylomorphic and theriomorphic.They are representations of *agwụ* as an individualized and personalized entity which embodies several attributes, quite often in opposition. This chapter also examines the relation between the world of men and that of the spirits through observing the existence and use of certain symbols in both worlds. The approach to the study of these symbols offers the chance for gaining a lot of insight into the nature of *agwụ* and human religious inclinations and thought.

Chapter Four focuses on the main institutions that are primarily under the patronage of *agwụ* and through which human beings receive *agwụ* force and become *dibịa*. A comparative examination of initiation rites of some subcultural areas enables one to appreciate in depth the great ritual wealth of the cult of *agwụ*. Several themes under which the multi-dimensional transformation of the initiate are articulated are presented as interpretational guidelines. The repetition of some facts is the result of the methodological approach by which we examine versions of a system with many things in common.

The meaning of the initiation to *'dibịahood'*, for those who exercise the functions of priest-diviners and physicians is examined in Chapter Five. The transformative effects on the *dibịa*, in its several aspects, are investigated alongside the tradition of training of those who have the vocation to the special ministries.

Chapter Six explores the effect of socio-cultural changes on the dogma of *agwụ* and attempts to explain the reasons for the modified forms of *agwụ* cult practices in the contemporary society. It tackles the uneasy question of the significance of the continued application of *agwụ* force by contemporary religious therapists.

4 The Agwụ Deity In Igbo Religion

Methodology

Theoretical Conceptualization of the Problem

Northcote W.Thomas (1913) identified *agwụ* as a mischievcus deity of Igbo religion, who could spoil farm products and who at the same time is recognized as tutelary deity of doctors.[2] Basden had also observed the traditional practices in matters of health-care and noted that while medicine is administered to the sick, sacrifices are offered to the gods.[3] In more recent times, scholarly works by F. Arinze, M. A. Onwuejeogwu and Ikenga-Metuh have reaffirmed the existence of such healing practices in the Igbo communities of even contemporary times. These authors have provided more clarifications on the relationship of *agwụ*, the *dibịa* and human sickness.

A systematic elaboration of a theologico-anthropological significance of *agwụ* certainly requires examination of the related myths and a field study of the symbols, rituals, religious persons and other means by which this deity manifests itself in the world of men. It is the task of this research work to illuminate as much as possible the many *agwụ*-related perplexing human-conditions and eventually bring about more understanding of the subject. Such understanding is crucial for continued dialogue and interaction with other religious and cultural systems.

Objective of Study

The work is aimed at studying the phenomenon, *agwụ*, as it is found in the various subcultural areas of Igbo society. The study includes not only the entity, *agwụ*, as a religious reality but also the intense anthropocentric interrelations with which it is

---

2   Northcote W. Thomas, *Law and Custom of the Ibo of Awka Neighbourhood S*. Nigeria. Harrison and Sons, London, 1913, p.28. The word *dibịa* is both the singular and the plural form. In most cases the context makes it clear enough which number is intended. The plural prefix *ndị (ndị dibịa)* indicates the plural form which some authors prefer to use.

3   G.T. Basden, *Among the Ibos of Nigeria*. University Publishing Edition, Lagos, 1982 p.224. First published in 1920.

associated. The comparative approach allows the revisiting of some theories and hypotheses applied in the study of traditional religion.

Agwụ is distinguished from other deities of Igbo religion because it reveals itself to man within human kinship and genetic structures. Hence, it is described as *'apụpa ahụ n'ọbara'* (of ones flesh and blood), for in most cases, one's *agwụ* is *agwụ nna (agwụ* of paternal family), *agwụ nne (agwụ* of maternal family) or *agwụ ụwa (agwụ* of reincarnation). This work explores this rare characteristic and seeks to discover its full theological and sociological import.

The study examines *agwụ* as a major culprit in the traditional conception of disease causation. This is most evident in what is referred to as *agwụ* possession, which, particularly in its first and negative stage, could manifest in several forms of sicknesses.

To arrive at a harmonious *agwụ*-human relationship, initiation into the cult is indispensable. The spiritual and social results of the rites are expressed in rich symbolisms. Initiation is the only means for obtaining *agwụ* powers used by diviners and physicians. The rites of initiation will be examined in detail to expc e the process of transformation through which the individual becomes a recipient of supernatural power. Finally, we shall examine the fate of *agwụ* in modern and Christian society.

Significance of Study

Agwụ is the patron spirit of the diviner and the physician and therefore, it is important in the understanding of the traditional system of health care. The system recognizes both the natural and religious dimensions of sickness. More than at any other time, the need to study the disease aetiology and healing systems of the traditional societies with a view to developing them has become more increasingly identified. A reappraisal of African traditional health care has become necessary in the situation of soaring cost of medical care in the world. A most

recent call in this direction has been made by the Swiss
theologian and Professor of Mission, J. Hollenweger:

> One of the most important contributions to the ecumenical movement
> is the African tradition of healing. It is well known that our western
> medical technology is only available to the rich in Africa. The World
> Health Organization and a number of mission societies therefore plead
> for cooperation between European medicine and certain aspects of
> traditional healing in Africa. This is not only vital for Africa. It is also
> important for the West. The time is fast approaching when we will run
> out of funds for our health industry. Most of what Africans say about
> health and illness is confirmed by far-seeing Western health specialists.
> We do not become ill all by ourselves, the community has an important
> role to play in health and sickness. Many illnesses have social and
> socio-psychological causes. Consequently, they should not only be
> tackled at the biological and biophysical level. The human and
> ecological context is just as important. That is why many Churches are
> rediscovering the liturgy of prayer and anointing for the sick. This is an
> area which cries out for more thoughtful theological treatment.[4]

Although this study does not claim to cover details of the
healing practices in the traditional society, it is certain that the
religious aspect of the practices which are based on the dogma of
agwụ may not be critically appreciated unless that dogma has
been well understood. Therein lies the importance of this work.

A critical appreciation of the dogma of *agwụ* is necessary, as
the traditional tendency of regarding some types of sicknesses
as afflictions of *agwụ* still exists in the present society. When
sickness is explained as divine wrath, the victim is seen as
bearing the burden of divine judgement, a view that is not likely
to sustain deep concern and sympathy for the sick. What is
equally true is that most Christian healing homes adopt an
eclectic approach such that most forms of religious therapies are
undergirded by both indigenous religious and Christian world-
views. The implications can easily be appreciated

Scope of Study

With regard to the subject matter, the study intends to focus on
the phenomenon *agwụ*, as a popular religious reality, as a spirit

---

4   J. Hollenweger, "Foreword" In Jacob K. Olupoma and Sulayman S. Nyang,
     (Eds.), *Religious Plurality in Africa: Essays in Honour of John S. Mbiti*.
     Mouton de Gruyter, Berlin, 1993, p.xi.

ïorce, as the object of a complex ritual system, as a dynamic element of Igbo religious history, and as a subjective experience of various individuals. *Agwụ* is recognized as belonging to the supernatural class of beings that constitute the object of human devotion. Subjectively, *agwụ* is a reality of individual human persons.
It is not a communal deity. It depends on persons rather than communal traditions for its manifestation, propagation and perpetuation in the world. Subjective experiences, therefore, constitute major ingredients in the definition of *agwụ*. As part of Igbo religious history, belief in *agwụ* has evolved through myths, folklore and the socio-religious institutions whose values include man's dynamic contest with disease, suffering and cosmic dread. The study appreciates *agwụ*, as a ritual system through which the human being is transformed into some divine instrument that enables him to gain access to divine knowledge and power. In that case, the study dwells extensively on the hermeneutics of *agwụ* symbols.

As regards the area to be covered by this study, the Igbo area of Southeast Nigeria constitutes the delimitation. There was, however, little hesitation in referring to facts outside this geographical area which serve the comparative objective of the work.

Theoretical Approach

We find the phenomenological approach suitable in this study for it enables us to investigate the matter in depth and objectively. Although a spectrum of nuances or varieties of this approach do exist, Rudolf Otto is one of the first to apply it with great success to the study of religion.[5]

Basically, phenomenology calls for a new approacn to the concretely experienced phenomenon. It demands that the scientist, as much as possible should try to isolate phenomena from presuppositions and describe them as faithfully as possible.

---

[5] Cf. Rudolf Otto, *The Idea of the Holy*. Oxford University Press, London, 1923, (Rep. 1982).

Previous beliefs about the reality must· be subdued. The approach demands that in exploring the reality, both as dogma and fact of human experience, one must as much as possible prevent the intervention of preconceptions. It requires of us to avoid the imposition of rational interpretations and try to see the reality as the owners themselves do. These are aspects of applying the bracketing principle which this approach demands. Among other benefits, the phenomenological approach offers greater opportunity for understanding the interrelatedness of the varieties of *agwụ* symbols.

Field Work

The research design adopted in this work is the comparative sample survey. Its adoption is necessitated by the very vast area covered by the study. In view of that, Igboland is stratified into four subcultural zones: North, South, East and West. In each area, specific communities are selected for study. Some factors were influential in the selection. The first is the popularity of a community in relation to *agwụ* cult practices, and such popularity is based on the number of *agwụ* devotees and experts in it. The second is that the structures and practices of the traditional religion have undergone only superficial changes and hence the phenomenon of *agwụ* is found very much intact. The third important consideration is the overall religious importance of the community. That is why such places as Nri and Arochukwu, important religious centres, are chosen. From each community, we made sure that the most popular or prominent *agwụ* specialist was interviewed, and the rest of those interviewed chosen by simple random method.

In each subcultural area, the number of *dibịa* chosen for interview were more or less, depending on the greater or lesser need of comparative materials for rechecking the reliability of data. There were two instances of group interviews. In either case, there was no prior notification of our visit. The first was at Nri in the house of Okereke Okonkwo who was at the time, the oldest man of the community. His son who is well educated and vastly informed on the religious and other cultural practices of Nri, and .another elder of the village, who is a member of the *agwụ* cult were present. The other instance was at Edda, in the house of Chief Ugbo Anuma, the Head of Edda traditional religion. It was *Eke* day, when Chief Anuma's cabinet, made up of heads of the various villages, was in session. Some of those present were members of *agwụ* cult, such as diviners and physicians. Some others were priests of other deities. It was possible to have a four hour discussion with this group. The discussion was very orderly and offered immediate opportunity for comparisons of data.

The data gathering involved oral interviews. Although we had formulated structured questions for this purpose, in actual interview sessions, it proved impossible to stick rigidly to them. A particular situation could require an informal interrogation which often proved useful.

Another method of data collection we employed was observation. The objects for observation included people possessed by *agwụ*, the shrines, *ụlọ agwụ (agwụ* house) or *ụlọ afa* (divination house), the several ritual symbols and the exercise of related services such as divination or healing.

Problems Encountered in Field Work

The field work researcher who has to meet and interview many unfamiliar people has need of a guide in the community under study. While that is primarily important, other factors may impede the progress of the work or enhance it. There is already traditional reticence towards strangers which increases with the *dibịa* who jealously guard the secrets of their profession. Our very first visit to a *dibịa* at the conceptual stage of the work is a typical case of failure. The *dibịa's* brother who is well known to me presented us to him and informed him that we desired to have some chat with him. When he found out that we had come not in search of his services but to inquire into the nature of his work, he informed us that on that market day, concerning the issue for which· we had come, he would not speak with us. We left and came back the following day as he had instructed only to be told by the wife that he was not going to see us on account of a sudden ill-health, which was very likely an affliction from his patron spirit, who was angry that he had given us an appointment. The message was clear. We left without another word.

The interview sessions were sometimes difficult even when the *dibia* was congenial and open but had to be allowed his habit of going through interminable digressions to answer simple and direct questions. At times we had to represent a question in several forms until we got such response that was consistent and reliable.

We did record many instances when the *dibia* refused absolutely to speak on some particular themes, knowledge of which was claimed, must remain the preserve of the ordained experts. In Edda community for example, Chima Ama doubted that any doctor worth his salt could divulge to non-initiates, such as ourselves, the identity of the herbs used during initiation of the *dibia*. When we mentioned some to him, he lamented the rising greed among some *dibia* who as a result, are ready to compromise the esoteric content of the system for a fee.

Coming to what he refers to as greed, our experience was that while many of the *dibia* did not demand to be paid any fees and accepted whatever gifts we presented in accordance with traditional courtesy, some others openly solicited for such gifts or asked for financial remuneration for the information we received justifying the same with such proverbs as: *"Anaghi agba aka agbafu nti"* (No one bores a hole in the ear bare-handedly) or *"anaghi agba aka ahu nwata eze"* (No one notices the child's teething with only words).

Each *dibia* observed some taboos especially for the *ulo agwu*. Strictness however, differed from one *dibia* to another. When we were not absolutely denied entry into the house, as was the case with Chima Ama, we were allowed on such conditions: to have no shoes on and to take no photographs. Permission to watch divination rituals was not always granted. We had though, the luck of meeting a few liberal diviners. In a certain case of oracular divination we got involved for the spirit promptly greeted us when she descended. The spirit, following the voice we heard was female and the *dibia* confirmed that. We responded to the spirit's greetings who inquired about our mission and wished us well. Most other diviners could only explain their practices to us. We were prepared for such problems and where it seemed unreasonable did not press too hard. We also obtained the services of interpreters where we were not quite conversant with a particular local dialect, as happened at Enugu-Ezike or at Illah. Our being Igbo was certainly of immense advantage for such a study. Again, the traditional hospitality which we encountered in most places helped to sustain our interest all through.

We had hoped when we set out on this research to witness, particularly, the main initiation rites into the cult of *dibiahood*. This remained unfulfilled for some reasons. First, the initiated members we had asked to invite us to any oncoming initiation rites did not do so. Only such people who are members of the cult easily get such information. Second, the frequency of such initiation rites has diminished with sociocultural and religious transformations that have been taking place for a century. Third, the original elaborate rites are today easily modified to accommodate the contemporary situation. While the accounts of initiation rites by those who have been initiated are to be relied upon, the researcher is more deeply touched when he is an eye witness.

Chapter 1

Supernaturalism And Disease Causation

Worlds in Contact

Most traditional or non-modern world-views admit the existence of the visible and natural world of men and the invisible and supernatural world of spiritual beings. The Igbo people entertain certain ambivalence as regards the distance between these worlds. Igbo folklore depicts a large volume of space between the two with the legendary number, seven. It is said that the traveller from one world to the other crosses 'seven deserts and seven seas'. It is the idea of an immense span of space.

This land of the spirits is also the place where the dead go. The dead must not try to reach it on an empty stomach. Hence, the regret when people died before they could eat, for then they would be lacking the strength to accomplish the journey successfully. It was also to provide sustenance for the journey that food was interred along with the dead, a practice that was popular in traditional funeral rites.

The vision of a dichotomized and well distanced cosmos however, is blurred by other human experiences. There is the immediacy and force that characterize man's experiences of the other world. The beings of the other world are invisible because they are always hiding in the bush and forest, behind trees, rocks and hills from where they quickly react to people's situations. How then could the world of the spirits be far removed from that of human beings if that were the case?

The interactions between the two worlds are so enormous that the boundaries could be said to overlap. Hiebert thus describes this overlapping perception: "There is no sharp distinction between the natural and the supernatural. Gods and spirits are as real in everyday experience as natural objects."[1] This is the supernaturalistic world-view which articulates a spiritualized universe, whose worlds then are hardly distinguished from one another. The proximity of the invisible world is further reassured by its ethical relation to the world of men in its being the major source of norms in the latter, norms which are taken to have been pronounced by spiritual beings such as ancestors and gods.

Again, the idea of the imperfect division of the natural and the supernatural worlds was in earlier times strengthened by such human experiences as sleep, waking, trance, dreams, echoes, visions etc. In these experiences people believed they came into contact with the other world and they did so without recording physical distance. Dreams are particularly effective, for it is in the world of dreams that men encounter the spirits of the other world. They believed that "the dead return in dreams, during sleep the soul wanders in the realm of the dead."[2] In dreams and other extraordinary experiences, the other world is often revealed in form and content as similar to the natural world. With such human experiences, belief in the proximity of the other world was easily sustained. The consequence according to Skorupski is that;

> a traditional religious cosmology, then extends the social field - and thus also the pattern of social relationship - beyond its members. In doing so, it extends the scope of interaction and operative ceremonies.[3]

The supernaturalistic world-view of the Igbo is centred on *Chukwu* (God) to whom the invisible world of gods and spirits, as well as the visible world of men, animals and plants owe their origin. In the popular creative myths, in folklore and religious rituals, God (the supreme being) is portrayed as omnipotent,

---

1   Paul G. Hiebert, *Cultural Anthropology*, J.B. Lippincott, Philadelphia, 1979, p.358.

2   Mircea Eliade, *Symbolism, the Sacred. the Art*, Crossroad, New York, 1986, p.60. In present times, the belief is not uncommon that some dreams bring some people in actual contact with their future experiences in the real world.

3   John Skorupski, *Symbol and Theory*, Cambridge University Press, Cambridge, 1976, p.166.

transcendent, provident, omniscient.[4] God's rulership of the world is discharged through the minor supernatural beings. These agents are conceived by some as emanations of God, as his servants and far more than he himself, are the immediate objects of worship. These agents include *Ala*, (the earth goddess), *Igwe* (the sky god), *Anyanwụ* (the sun god) and *Amadịoha/Kamalụ* (the god of thunder). These are symbolized with natural phenomena of universal extensions. *Ala*, and *Amadịoha* have elaborate cults and priestly orders. *Ala*, particularly has a cult that is well diffused and she provides the basis of the entire moral code as well as the idiom in the definition of social identity and solidarity. Infringement on a grave prohibition is called *ụrụ ala*, (polluting the earth).[5]

In all parts of Igboland, there are deities that reflect particular physical characteristics of the place, such as streams, hills, forests, valleys or plain land. There are always myths that narrate the mysterious origin of such features and these have made them into symbols of spiritual realities.

There are deities that have been established by the ancestors of communities for specific purposes. The reason may be to protect the town and its people, or to enhance the flourishing of the markets. Deities may originate when traumatic events such as the outbreak of some epidemic or war occurs. To institute a deity for the community, a stock from the one that is desired is taken and installed, or a *dibịa*(medicine-man) is invited to 'make medicine' which is placed in the town and around which a divine cult develops. The 'birth' or institution of a god is brought about in such circumstances.[6] No matter the conditions of their origin,

---

4   An elaborate treatment of God's attributes in Igbo religion is found in Emefie Ikenga-Metuh, *God and Man in African Religion*, Geoffrey Chapman, London, 1981, p.33ff. Igbo theophoric names also abundantly express such attributes.

5   For details on the subject of prohibitions and pollution in Igbo society see, Jude C.U. Aguwa, "Taboos and Purification of Ritual pollutions in Igbo Traditional Society: Analysis and Symbols." *Anthropos* 88(1993): 539 - 546.

6   Chinua Achebe in *Arrow of God* tells about the origin of the town, Umuaro as well as their deity, *Ulu*. According to this account, in order to halt the attacks

deities and spirits are, however, believed to be created by God and generally taken to be his agents.

The Igbo pantheon contains a category of supernatural beings whose interests centre around man and his activities. They are essentially departmental gods or spirits that govern the many phases of nature and human life as well as the progress of human activities. They are known to be capable of promoting or hindering human welfare, of advancing or ruining man's undertakings and to reverse their actions or stop them from inflicting harm, man must have recourse to sacrifices. There are deities that patronize farm work, protect habitations, give fertility to women, assist in war and superintend the health department. Evil spirits that account for human negative experiences are felt to be present in most of man's daily activities. As Skorupski puts it, "one finds the reality of gods and spirits woven with many strands of belief into everyday experience."[7]

Agwy is the patron spirit of herbal medicine and divination. It also inspires intellectual and artistic activities as well as many other human values. Those who initiate fully into the cult become priests (*dibia-aja*), physicians (*dibia-ogwy*) and diviners (*dibia-afa*). *Agwy* makes its intrusion in the lives of people through a whole lot of effects which are initially negative and may later be replaced by positive ones when the human party meets divine will with appropriate response.

The everyday references to gods and spirits in the very many spheres of human existence and in the many occupations have created the view of a universe though dichotomized, is so only

---

and harassments of Abam soldiers, six villages came together. They decided and "hired a strong team of medicine-men to install a common deity for them. This deity was called *Ulu*. Half of the medicine was buried at a place which became *Nkwo* market and the other half thrown into the stream which became *Mili Ulu*. The six villages then took the name Umuaro, and the priest of *Ulu* became their Chief Priest. From that day they were never again beaten by an enemy. (p. 14-15). Achebe also narrates the story of the *Eke* market of Okperi which had suffered great decline: "Then one day the men of Okperi made a powerful deity and placed their market in its care. From that day *Eke* grew and grew until it became the biggest market in these parts" Cf *Arrow of God*, Heinemann, 1974 (first published in 1964) p.19

[7] John Skorupski *Symbol and Theory*, p.26.

imperfectly, as the beings of the supernatural world can suspend or enhance the processes in the natural world.

A g w ụ : Etymological Perspective

Agwụ patronizes the *dibịa* in his use of *ọgwụ*. *Ọgwụ* describes a spectrum of phenomena which are used to cure sickness or to bring it about. It may be provided to act as a protection against malevolent and angry spirits, their agents, or other inimical abstract forces. *Agwụ* is the patron deity of both medicine and magic and the word *ọgwụ* is used to describe both practices. Hence, the word *ọgwụ* is a generic term for medicinal herbs and materials, charms, preparations and any other substances that man uses to save and protect his life and the acts he performs to exercise control of supernatural forces . There is apparently a derivational relationship between the words *agwụ* and *ọgwụ* which would point to a deeper reality of intrinsic connection between the two realities the terms represent.

Other names by which *agwụ* is known are *a g w ụisi* (agwụishi) and *agwụnsị*. The suffixes *isi* and *nsị* literally and respectively mean head/first and poison. Their usages are more or less popular in one subcultural area or the other. The etymological difference between them arose from the fact that they emphasize different attributes of *agwụ*. But the term *agwụ* on its own is much more universally used and understood with the full attributes of the deity.

The term *agwụisi* may be traced to four possible contexts of origin. In the first place, *agwụisi* underlines the key role which *agwụ* plays in the spirit world, as their spokesman. It is said that "All *alụsị* manifest their will through the *alụsị* called *agwụ* that determine the fall of the diviner's beads in *afa* divination."[8] *Agwụ*, it is also believed , monitors the designs of other spirits and deities including *Chukwu* and reveals these to humans in divination. It is also through *agwụ* that the inhabitants of the spirit world make their wishes known in the natural world. *Agwụ* determines the remedies for an angry or disgruntled

---

8   M.A. Onwuejeogwu, *An Igbo Civilization: Nri Kingdom and Hegemony*, Ethiope Publishing Corporation, London, 1981. p.36.

spirit. **Such privileged functions** have earned *agwụ* the prominence of 'spokesman' and status of a sort of head in the spirit world.[9]

Secondly, *agwụisi* refers to *ara-agwụ*, the mental disorder believed to be punishment for one who refuses to become a votary of the *agwụ* cult. Since this malady is located in the head, the traditional mind articulated the association with the expression *agwụisi* (*agwụ* of the head).

Thirdly, the term *agwụisi* may have originated from the arrangement of the traditional liturgical calendar. *Agwụ* festival takes place in the fifth lunar month which in parts of traditional Igbo society, such as Nri, is the beginning of the year. Thus, the feast comes up as the first in the liturgical calendar.

Fourthly, the tradition of experience shows that of all the known supernatural beings, *agwụ* makes the earliest intrusion into people's lives. For this reason, *agwụ* is described as "*ihe mbụ na-eme tupu ndi ọzọ ewere bịa*" (the event after which others follow). This also explains why *agwụ* is the divinity of *Eke*, the first day of Igbo weekday and people born on this day are called *Ekeagwụ*.

On the other hand, the term *agwụnsị* (*agwụ*, the poison) provokes thoughts of the ability of *agwụ* to produce effects as severe and destructive as poison. In this sense, the term *agwụ* is the metaphor for several negative qualities which human beings exhibit. Those who are antisocial, queer, prone to aggressiveness or to crimes are often regarded as *ndi agwụ* (*agwụ* people). So also are those who are very stubborn, uncompromising and inclined to interminable litigations. *Agwụ* initial advances are generally afflictive and would change later only when certain conditions have been fulfilled. Taken together, *agwụisi* and *agwụnsị* serve the complementary role of providing the enigmatic picture of the reality, *agwụ*.

---

9 In that sense *agwụ* is similar to the patron spirit of divination, *Fa*, among the Ewe in Benin, Togo and Ghana, which is known to reveal the will of the supreme god (*Mawụ*) as it affects human destiny. Since *Fa* understands the languages of other deities it normally mediates in their relationship with men. Particularly in that role it is the patron spirit of diviners.

The Many Faces of *Agwụ*

Since the world of spirits is thought to be similar to that of men, *agwụ is* considered not to be a single entity but a plurality. Human attributes in such areas as gender, ethics, social relations are projected into the world of the gods. In other words, the visible world is a reflection of the world of the spiritual beings. Traditional religious thought tends to personify the manifestations of *agwụ* which are affirmed in the varying ecologies or environments and in the many areas of human engagements. Individuals, therefore, have *agwụ* which may be attributed with many of such characteristics.

Genealogical
Agwụ nna - of the agnate line
Agwụ nne - of the enate line
Agwụ ụwa - of reincarnation

Gender
Oke agwụ - the male that causes insanity
Nwunye agwụ - the female spirit that can increase fertility in
women

Agwụ nyama- possesses only women

Ethico-ontological
Agwụ oma - this is benevolent in nature
Agwụ ojọọ - this is malevolent in nature

Environment
Agwụ ụlọ - has its shrine erected in the vicinity of the home
Agwụ ohịa - has its shrine erected in the bush

Grades of Power
Agwụ ukwu - the great *agwụ*
Agwụ nta - the small *agwụ*

Specialization and Occupation
Agwụ dibịa-possesses doctors
Agwụ afa - possesses diviners

maleficent do, as a matter of natural behaviour, afflict human beings and other creatures in the world with harm.

Gods and spirits respond to human evil conduct by punishing the offender with sickness. The perpetrator of evil in the family and in the community earns the wrath of the ancestors who inflict the person with sickness. The breaking of taboos cause sickness if the appropriate ritual purifications and propitiation rites are not undertaken.[14] Human beings such as witches or sorcerers who possess supernatural powers cause sickness in other people. Foster describes such sickness as personalistic since;

> aggression or punishment is directed against a single person as a consequence of the will and power of a human being or supernatural agent or being.[15]

Being the patron spirit of the diagnostician and physician *agwụ* plays a key role in the articulation of traditional disease aetiology. But the spirit is even involved at another level since it is the cause of human sickness of diverse forms. Works by

---

[14] Cf. Jude C. U. Aguwa, "Taboos and Purification of Ritual Pollutions in Igbo Traditional Society: Analysis and Symbolism." *Anthropos* 88 (1993): 539 - 546.

[15] G.N.Foster, "An Introduction to Ethnomedicine", in R.H. Bannerman, J.Burton, C.W.Wen,(Editors) *Traditional Medicine and Health Care Coverage*, WHO, Geneva, 1983, p.19. Christensen's study of the Fanti priesthood of Southern Ghana exemplifies the interpretation affirming the supernatural causes of diseases. According to him: "Divination usually reveals that the supernatural is in some manner involved in the patient's illness. With the very broad range of obligations to the supernatural, in the fulfillment of which the client may have been lax, and with the possibility that he is being punished for having broken a secular rule of conduct, the cause of an affliction may literally be any one of hundreds. An ancestor may be showing displeasure because the terms of his *samansew* (a will, given orally before death) were not properly observed. It may be that some personal property, such as a cherished piece of jewelry, that he had directed should be interred with him was retained by the family; a sister's son that he had designated as his heir may have been passed over in favour of another kinsman; some aspect of a required funerary rite may have been neglected." Cf. James Boyd Christensen, "The Adaptive Functions of Fanti Priesthood", William R. Bascom and Milville J. Herskovits, (editors), *Continuity and Change in African Cultures*. University of Chicago Press, Chicago, 1965, p.262.

authors such as Arinze, Ilogu, Awolalu and Dopamu, Onwuejeogwu, Ikenga-Metuh and Ifeanyi have elaborated on the relationship of sickness, *agwu*, and the *dibia*.[16]

One of the earliest studies on the subject by the anthropologist, Northcote W. Thomas, has clearly noted the prankish tendencies of *agwu*:

> ... and we have *Agu* [*Agwu*], who really comes much closer to the evil spirits than to the demi-gods, for though a demi-god requires to be propitiated, he does not appear to act malevolently of his own free will. If any one suffers from his anger it is because of some infraction of his privileges, such as unauthorized entry into his sacred bush. *Agu* [*agwu*], on the other hand, is a mischievous spirit who will spoil the yams and other crops and bring unlimited misforture upon any one that he chooses to play his pranks on .... It is perhaps a little singular that *Agu* [*agwu*] is a sort of tutelary deity of the doctors. If he pursues with misfortune an ordinary individual until the limit of his patience is reached and no remedy can be found, it is a sign that the man should become doctor.[17]

This is to say that in the act of possessing the *dibia*, *agwu* accounts for many traditionally identified human negative conditions . Arinze has correctly observed that:

> the clearest and indispensable sign of vocation to be a *dibia* i s possession by the spirit *agwu*, who is the special spirit of *ndi dibia*, the spirit of giddiness, rascality, discomposure, confusion and forgetfulness (*mmuo mkpasa uche*).[18]

The spirit, *Agwu*, is regarded as one of God's agents and that is why it is said that "the knowledge of medicine came directly from God and it operates through the tutelary divinities

---

16 F.A. Arinze, *Sacrifice in Ibo Religion;* E. Ilogu, *Christianity and Igbo Culture*, NOK Publishers, London, 1974; J. Awolalu & P. Adelumo Dopamu, *West African Traditional Religion;* M.A. Onwuejeogwu, *An Igbo Civilization: Nri Kingdom and Hegemony;* Emefie Ikenga-Metuh, *God and Man in African Religion;* Victor Ifeanyi, *The Catholic Church and the Challenges of Traditional System of Health Care in Nigeria*. Rome, 1989.

17 Northcote W. Thomas, *Law and Custom of the Ibo of the Awka Neighbourhood S. Nigeria*, pp.27-28.

18 F. A. Arinze, *Sacrifice in Ibo Religion*, p.64. See also M.A. Onwuejeogwu, *An Igbo Civilization: Nri Kingdom and Hegemony*, p.34.

or spirits."[19] The Igbo commonly express this idea in the saying: *Chukwu kere dibịa, kere ọgwụ* (It is God who has created both the physician and the medicine).

Our study so far has shown that there is apparently a vital relationship between the world of men and that of the spirits. In fact, it would appear that the survival of either of them depends on their mutual co-existence. In isolation, each provides only but little and temporary contentment or fulfillment. Hence, the vigorous traffic between them, when gods come to the human world to exercise power and to consume sacrifices, and when men die and seek the bliss of ancestorhood in the world of the dead. The content of *agwụ* dogma discloses that *agwụ* is vitally present in the human world and in human life-experiences. This is the theme of the next chapter.

---

[19] T.N.O. **Quarcoopome**, *West African Traditional Religion*, African University Press, **Ibadan**, 1987, p.147.

Chapter 2

The Anthropocentricity Of *Agwụ*

Agwụ appears to exercise its influence over the various aspects of human life and activities more than most other gods of the Igbo pantheon. The vital areas of health and sickness fall under its superintendence. The obvious consequence of this is that, at one time or the other, most people would come to need *agwụ* through the professional services of the *dibịa*. Those who make outstanding achievements in creative art and oratory; people who successfully undertake adventures; those who succeed in their careers; people who are valiant, influential and wealthy; attribute most of that to the patronage of *agwụ*.

The existence of many symbols of *agwụ* point to its extensive influences. Myths of *agwụ* origin and the stories of its epiphany or manifestation in the world of men are well diffused. There are myths too, of the transmission of the *agwụ* spirit and power from one person to the other and well recognized symptoms of possession of persons by *agwụ*. There is a rich onomastic build-up deriving from *agwụ* dogma and cult practices. As we study these aspects, the anthropocentricity of *agwụ* is discovered as a well articulated perspective in Igbo traditional theology.

The Myth of *Mmụọ* and *Agwụ*

According to this myth-

> *Chukwu* had the appearance of a pair of siamese giants one of which had masculine figure and was called *mmụọ* while the other figure had feminine appearance and was called *agwụ*. The two figures of *Chukwu* were joined at the buttocks facing opposite directions. *Mmụọ*, the masculine face of *Chukwu* was always benevolent and did only good. *Agwụ* was always malevolent and did only evil. After *Chukwu* had created earth and after the earth had solidified, God used to descend to earth for recreation. Because *agwụ* was continually drawing *Mmụọ* back and retarding his progress, *Chukwu* pulled out his bones with which he

25

made his first group of sons whom he called 'Oji'... Chukwu drained agwu's blood and with it formed his second group of men ... Chukwu pulled out Agwu's intestine and with these he created the 'Edo' group of people ... Then mmuo pulled out agwu's head which he left on the ground to become 'Ani' - the earth goddess. Having thus relieved himself of agwu, Chukwu flew back into the sky and from there he controls the earth till this day[1]

The myth of mmuo and agwu, is essentially a creation myth. Agwu was not an accidental instrument in the hands of mmuo. He shared divine nature with mmuo and was his other face. He stands in opposition to mmuo [Chukwu] in the contest of good against evil and the former is seen to prevail. The contest does not however, seem to be over. Even so agwu was not essentially negative for it contributed the substance with which Chukwu created the races of men as well as the gods. Agwu was not destroyed but transmuted. Our interest in this story is the possible light it throws on the understanding of the agwu phenomenon and dogma even today. There are such issues as the gender of agwu, its malevolent attributes, its human centredness, its special relation to other gods, which can be fruitfully discussed in the light of this myth.

The Human Origin of Agwu

Based on the ethico-ontological perceptions by which agwu ojoo is distinguished from agwu oma, the origins of the two types or aspects of agwu have been explained with differentiated hypotheses of their human origins.

The Human Origin of Agwu Ojoo

The origin of agwu ojoo (negative/bad agwu) is attributed to human ex-corporate spirits. These are persons who during their earthly lives fall short of social and moral expectations, or who commit abominations by dying of certain diseases, on account of which they are denied proper funerary rites. The consequence of denial of such rites is that the spirits of such dead persons do not

---

[1]   I.N.C. Nwosu, The Ndi Ichie Akwa Mythology, quoted in Catherine O. Acholonu, "Folklore Origins of the Igbos", Nigeria Magazine, vol. No. 55, No. 4, Oct - Dec. 1987 p.73. Nwosu is from Nnewi and the myth likely originated from that area.

reach the bliss of ancestors. They eventually gang up according to their earthly lineage units to harass the living members of their families. These are *agwu ojoo* or *mmuo ojoo* (evil spirits). This hypothesis gives two outstanding indications concerning the nature of *agwu*, namely, that *agwu* imitates the human social structure in the determination of its identity, and, that individual ex-corporate spirits cannot be *agwu*. *Agwu* is a cabal, a collection, a legion with only a group identity. The solidarity in a common purpose, of those of a particular human social unit is the binding force of these unfulfilled and disgruntled spirits.[2]

The Human Origin of Agwu oma

Agwu oma (the positive, benevolent and good *agwu*) differs from *agwu ojoo* in origin, nature and purpose. It is the collective and determined will of family founders to secure for themselves and their progenies that advantage by which they could maintain monopoly in matters of economic value such as medicine, divination and artistic practices. This collective will is ritually translated into spiritual and dynamic force that through the generations reasserts its objective, and by that, maintains its continuity in the family.[3] It is this spiritual force, which accounts for the endurance and heredity of certain professions, notably

---

2   On moral grounds some categories of people are disqualified to become ancestors. Ezekwugo calls them *ekwensu* - "wicked disembodied spirits who for one reason or the other are refused entry into the land of the dead.. and now wander about on earth causing accidents and misfortune, illness and sudden or premature deaths, instigating evil deeds and trying to push men into trouble. They are people who in their life time were perpetrating wicked deeds like witchcraft, robbery and murder, people who lived lawless lives and hated their fellow men... wicked men make wicked spirits. Curiously enough, the Igbos also hold that even those good men who do not receive ritual burial after their death do not reach their *Chi's* home; they keep roaming about in the vicinity of men and after some time turn wicked and thus become *ekwensu*." (Cf. Christopher U.M. Ezekwugo, *Chi the true God in Igbo Religion*, Pontifical Institute of Philosophy and Theology, Alwaye, Kerela, India, 1987, p.167.) In Nri and some parts of Igboland, *ekwensu* is clearly identified as the *agwu*.

This explanation was given at Nri during an interview granted by Okereke Okonkwo. His son, Ambrose Okonkwo and some other elders who were present made immense contributions. Okereke Okonkwo is already 90 years old and is the oldest man in Nri.

medicine and divination, within the family. The force, *agwu*, is then a religious institution that has existed from time immemorial. The ancients who established it had to ordain certain rituals in the form of sacrifices. These rituals enable the spiritual force to be sustained and transmitted through the generations. Sometimes, there would be negligence on the part of the progenies that leaves *agwu* starved of food. *Agwu* visits such careless inheritors with many afflictions to arouse them from their slumber.

The Anthropomorphic Epiphany of *Agwu*

The manifestation of *agwu* in human form is another mythological narrative that was quite diffused in most parts of Igboland. According to one version;

> *Agwu* was born as a human being
> And it abounded in deformities
> It was a monster and an *aru* (abomination)
> Its abnormal hands and feet were bound together and
> It was carried away into the evil forest
> But before those who carried it away came back
> *Agwu* was once again back in the house . . . [4]

An indication that this myth was widespread in ancient Igboland is the practice, still extant, of alluding to cases of severe birth deformities as *agwu* or *agwu* reincarnation.

The status of this myth is illuminated by other practices in ancient Igbo society. Twins were discarded and exposed because they were considered as abomination. Dwarfs who were abnormal human beings were rejected except in Nri community where they enjoyed high ritual valorization. The monster child was seen as an aberration and was assigned the same fate as twins. The myth recounts the mysterious return of this monster and the ability it had to impose itself formidably and absolutely, which proved its supernatural nature.

---

4   This account was given by Akunne, the attendant at Odinani Museum at Nri during an interview. Several Igbo myths have been recovered from this community, (Cf. M.A. Onwuejeogwu, *An Igbo Civilization: Nri Kingdom and Hegemony).*

Agwu - A Personal deity

Agwu is a personal deity. Men and women devotees have their individual shrines. The men build theirs at the entrance to the family compound while the women have theirs in front of the kitchen or behind it. *Agwu* does not receive communal veneration and there are no communal shrines to it. This situation obtains although many communities have in their ritual calendars, periods when those properly initiated as *dibia* and others who are devotees celebrate feasts in honour of their respective *agwu*. Each person offers what he could afford, a chicken or goat. One could invite one's friends and neighbours to share in the food and drinks.

In some places the feast acquires some semblance of a communal celebration when there are some public demonstrations of magical powers by particular masquerades or members of the league of the *dibia* in the community. Such activities even when so organized do not amount to public worship for there is no public shrine to *agwu*. In Nri community, for instance, the fifth lunar month (which is reckoned in the traditional calendar as the beginning of the year) is normally *onwa agwu* (the month of *agwu*). It is a feast 'to let *agwu* loose' (*itohapu agwu*). Masquerades display their art with the frenzy and rascality which are believed to be characteristic of this deity. They simulate *agwu* perceived as negative force, as spirit of violence and war. When *agwu* is let free, it is like reversing the rite of initiation (*iru agwu*) by which it is put under control in order to check its excesses and harness its positive powers.

In Amangwu community, the annual feast in honour of *agwu*, is called *ikoro agwu*, and it takes place in the month of September. The *dibia* of this area gather during the feast and display magic and wonder in public. In Ihechiowa, where the feast is also called *ikoro agwu* and celebrated in September, the leader of the guild of the *dibia* sacrifices a dog but shares the meat into four parts for the following: the custodian of his shrine (that is himself), the members of his lineage, the village, and the *dibịa* guild. In Agulu also, *onye bu isi agwụ* (the cult head in the community) could sacrifice a cow while other members use goats and fowls in their respective offerings. Since this is private worship there is no regulation about what one offers. Each devotee gives thanks to *agwụ* for any favours granted in the year and prays for the future.

In many other communities the *dibịa* and other votaries of *agwụ* celebrate in their families inviting members of the kindred to meals. When one's *agwụ* is matrilocal, the relatives from the maternal family are usually invited.

Part of the preparations for the feast include, clearing the weed at the shrine of *agwụ* and its vicinity, and decorating it with fresh palm twigs. The ritual plants at the shrine are also pruned when they have become overgrown. It is thereby said that *agwụ* has been given a haircut. The parts of the sacrificial items that belong to *agwụ* are placed at the shrine. Such feasts are believed to placate it and deter it from disturbing members of the community in the coming year.

There are villages referred to as *ndị ji isi agwụ* (Heads of the *agwụ* cult). They are recognized to have special relationship with *agwụ* and hence exercise some authority during initiation of new members from nearby villages. Such is the village *Ụmụagwụ* (children of *agwụ*) in Ezuhu Nguru. It is explained that it earned its name by having many prominent *dibịa* and also because it had a very high proportion of victims of *agwụ* negative influences.

The *agwụ* tradition of a village might become victim of an absolutely negative charaterization. This can affect her relationship with her neighbours. In Okigwe area for instance, people of Ụmụka do not usually marry from Ohengele, for according to the former, the women from there are carriers of *agwụ* force, whose malevolence has no rival and defies all known remedies. The fear persists till the present times but other villages around Ohengele do not share this view.

Transmission of *Agwụ*-Force

Agwụ is passed on from one individual to the other within a kindred. According to traditional explanations, the life of an individual is determined by elements which are paternal, maternal, reincarnational or that belong to the individual destiny. These are the keys to explain individual experiences and the means by which a person relates to his past and his future, to other human beings and even to the gods. They are channels or conduits through which spiritual power finds home in a person. The common belief is that a person's *agwụ*-force could derive from one or more of the following sources; the patrilineal or agnate source (*agwụ nna*), the matrilineal or enate source (*agwụ nne*), reincarnation (*agwụ so ọbịbịa ụwa*) and personal fate (*agwụ nke so chi*).

Transmission through Agnate and Enate lines
The belief is that *agwụ* is rooted in families and that is why it is described as, *apụpa na ọbara* (pertaining to flesh and blood) or as *ihe dị ebe ndị* (a thing in a family tradition). It is therefore, not a spirit extraneous to the family nor to the individual, but very well in the veins.[5] *Agwụ* is unlike an *arụsị* or *agbara* which is created to serve purposes of protection and which could also be discarded when its power fades. *Agwụ* follows the blood line because it is the banding of lineage spirits or because it is that spirit force that serves a particular family interest. *Agwụ* is taken to be inherited through the following sources: the patrilineal and the matrilineal. The likelihood that children take over the professions of the parents, especially those of the *dibịa* where *agwụ* makes the greatest impact reflects how strongly the dogma is held. Arinze'has explained that the facts of heredity and

---

5   In the recently published biography of Dr. Nwogu, Eberechukwu Anosike traces the medical tradition of Nwogu's family down to the fourth generation and makes the point that it was a matter of course that Dr. Nwogu became practitioner in both western medicine and ethnomedicine. Cf. Eberechukwu M. Anosike, *A Modern Healer: The life and Work of Dr. Cyril Ekenwa O. Nwogu*, Imo State University Press, Uturu, 1992, pp.1-3.

personal vocation in the case of *agwụ* possession are quite compatible:

> The office of the *dibịa* is largely hereditary. Particular families invariably perform the ceremonies of *agwụ* and tell fortune. This does not contradict the fact that possession is a necessary sign of vocation, for it almost always comes to a son of a *dibịa*, hence the saying *Ndị na-eme agwụ ka agwụ na-akpa* (It is those who minister to *agwụ* that *agwụ* possesses). *Agwụ* has no preference for the first-born son (*ọkpala*) as in the case of a priest. Sometimes the candidate is already known from boyhood when he picks up certain seeds called *mkpụlụ afa* (seeds for divining).[6]

Agwụ selects a devotee through the manifestation of one or several signs in the life of the individual. Practices obtain that at a man's death, any of the children selected, following the appearance of the signs, takes custody of the father's *agwụ* symbols such as, *ntụtụ agwụ*, *ekwụm agwụ*, *ọfọ agwụ*, etc. If one was still too young at the father's death, one would be expected to get initiated and exercise the appropriate ritual responsibilities on becoming an adult. Other members of the family must neither deprive the chosen the opportunity to respond to this calling nor try to usurp it. There are no liberties about whether one so chosen could take up the responsibility or not. It is believed that *agwụ* deals any delinquents, crushing blows.

When the *agwụ* tradition in a family is marked by a period of passivity, the signs of the awakening are usually regarded with skepticism. A visible display of the spirit's negative force might be required to convince those concerned of its reality. An informant whose family *agwụ* so behaved recounted a litany of vicissitudes he went through. He could hardly go half way through primary school. Sixteen years of trading in several towns were fraught with losses. When he returned home, and took to cutting palm fruits, frustrations of all types continued to unfold. He most often mistook the unripe for the ripe fruits. His marriage was marked by quarrels and ended in divorce. His farm crops were often destroyed by pests.

---

6   Francis A. Arinze, *Sacrifice in Ibo Religion*, p. 65.

At other times the harvests proved exceedingly poor even when he took great care in planting. When he started to hearken to the advice of diviners his fortunes witnessed a change for the better. We found his expressions of contentment with his present conditions quite justified judging by the state of development in his compound which testifies to a period of steady growth.[7] The common explanation given by diviners in this type of case is that *agwụ* could remain passive for such a period that generations might pass with no records of its presence. But some day it wakes up in search of its own and that is why it is said that *agwụ anaghị agbagha ụmụ ya* (*agwụ* does not forsake its children).

Transmission of Agwụ through Reincarnation

The passage of *agwụ* from one generation to another, from ancestors to living progenies is also achieved by the mechanism of reincarnation. The dogma of reincarnation maintains that ancestors come back to live in their earthly families within their lineages and could even do so among their friends. Such a name as *Nnanna* (grand father) or *Nnenne* (grand mother) which is given to a child is in keeping with the belief. A motive for ancestor veneration Nnadozie explains , is that "they reincarnate to perpetuate the clan they founded in their time."[8] "Some popular understanding of reincarnation in Igbo religious thought holds that ;

man does not die. Life does not end with death. An individual only 'goes home' from whence he came back when his shopping is done, to begin afresh his continuous cycle of birth, death, reincarnation on a similar, higher or lower level of existence depending on how he had lived his previous life. An individual, in Igbo cosmology, is expected to complete seven life cycles. He can return after death to start another cycle provided that he completed the previous cycle naturally. If he dies before the prescribed cycle is complete, then it means that the natural order has been interfered with. Such a person is likely to make more

7   The informant, Aja Kalu, from Arochukwu is a diviner and healer .

8   Josef Awazie Nnadozie, "Offspring (omụmụ) in Nguru Traditional Marriage: (A Sociological, Anthropological and Theological Investigation)"; Thesis for B.D., Bigard Memorial Seminary, Enugu, 1978, p. 7.

than seven rounds or cycles in order to realign his life to the cosmic order.[9]

Another aspect of belief in reincarnation is the possibility of two or more simultaneous reincarnations of the same ancestor. This has raised questions on whether an entity and a personality wholly reincarnates or does so in parts. The doctrine of reincarnation is further complicated by claims that the living are able to reincarnate. The name *Uwandu* (*idi n d u lo uwa*) expresses such belief. In the course of this study we witnessed this belief being often expressed and the explanation is that people who reincarnate while alive, count it as a sign of their generous disposition, just as one who effects multiple reincarnations, for the intention is to give out oneself to as many people as possible.

In reincarnation, sex and status changes are possible. A woman could reincarnate as a man and vice versa. A pauper could become a king. One's desires intensively uttered, especially from a background of the experience of severe human anguish and hardship are believed to be realizable in reincarnation. At the burial of successful parents, children charge them to return once again as their parents in the next cycle of their human existence.

The complexity of the belief in reincarnation is evident in the difficulty of reconciling the discrepancies in the dogma and the ritual practices. Nnadozie has suggested an answer which affirms a unity of a dual nature of the ancestor, where one nature could reincarnate while the other does not, and remains the constant object of veneration. According to him:

> ...the part of the ancestor that reincarnated and the part that remained in the patriarchal kingdom for worship were not distinct. There was the belief, however that any part of the dead ancestor could reincarnate to the son or the daughter he loved. As it were, his body-members were vegetatively reincarnatable while his soul rested with the gods of the forefathers in the patriarchal kingdom. At times in their local proof that an ancestor reincarnated the people left the impression of a hot-red signet on any part of the corpse. Incidentally a child born with a mark

---

9   Chinwe Achebe, *The World of the Ogbanje*, Fourth Dimension Publishers, Enugu, 1986, p. 17.

ahuwa-nma as they called it was said to be that forefather come back to life.[10]

Following this and similar explanations, there are biological or physiological characteristics which simply represent the reality of reincarnation. Psychological or behavioural character of a child, when found to be similar to those of the dead members of the lineage pointed to a dead person coming back to life. The belief was very firm in the minds of the people. In the novel, *Things Fall Apart*, Achebe puts the crude dogma in the mouth of an *Egwugwu* (masquerade) at the burial of Ezeudu:

> Ezeudu... if you had been poor in your last life I would have asked you to be rich when you come again. But you were rich. If you had been a coward, I would have asked you to bring courage. But you were a fearless warrior. If you had died young, I would have asked you to get life. But you lived long. So I shall ask you to come again in the way you came before.[11]

This address expresses the belief that biological and mental qualities are brought along in reincarnation and that reincarnation is also expected to lead one to fill up deficiencies of one's past life.

With regard to *Agwụ*, the Igbo say; *agwụisi bụ ihe eji alọ ụwa* (man reincarnates with *agwụ*). It is assumed that ancestors of both the patrilineal and the matrilineal families reincarnate and usually do so with the *agwụ* of their former lives. As they reincarnate to perpetuate their lineages, they bring *along* the *agwụ* of their families. When a person's reincarnation is agnate, then he has *agwụ nna*. It is *agwụ nne* when reincarnation is enate. Hence, reincarnation acts as the mechanism by which *agwụ* is perpetuated in the family lineage.

In some parts of western Igbo, such as Illah and Asaba, *ịlọ ụwa* (reincarnation) is synonymous with *ịlọ agwụ* (reincarnation of *agwụ*). It suggests the traditional association of the two.

---

10   Josef Awazie Nnadozie, "Offspring (ọmụmụ) in Nguru traditional Marriage: (A Sociological, Anthropological and Theological Investigation)", pp. 7-8.

11   Chinua Achebe, *Things Fall Apart*, Heinemann, London, 1958, rep. 1985, p. 85.

Agwụ ụwa (*agwụ* of reincarnation) in Enugu Ezike of northern Igbo, is also called *ọgwụ so mmadụ na ụwa ya* or *ọgwụ ọlụwa* (medicine that follows a person from reincarnation or destiny). We already have noted the etymological relationship between *ọgwụ* and *agwụ* and the fact that the latter is the patron spirit that patronizes the former. *Agwụ* is a spirit, so personal and so much part of the family that its transmission through reincarnation was perceived as logical.

Agwụ from Ritual Contagion and Indebtedness

Some individuals find themselves in a state of contagion in relation to *agwụ* when they consistently and deliberately partake of food or other things that have been offered to *agwụ* while remaining uninitiated into *agwụ* cult. The state of contagion manifests as a form of possession by which the victim is disturbed until he becomes a votary of *agwụ*, so that others could also have the chance for reciprocal treatment from him. In this way a person comes to recognize the *agwụ* of his family and to give it proper attention.

In the same predicament are those who steal property, such as livestock or tamper with the shrine or bush dedicated to *agwụ*. Such people become 'infected with the *agwụ* spirit force'. *Agwụ* visits them with chains of disturbances until restitution is made. It is said: *Agwụ biara madụ ụgwọ* (*agwụ* comes to be paid what it is owed). Should this debt not be paid in one's life time, reincarnation provides that unattended obligations of the former life be carried over to the next cycle of earthly existence. The *dibịa* in their diagnoses are able to distinguish *agwụ* that is so contracted. The victims are referred to as *ndị nyara akpa agwụ pụta ụwa* (those who enter the world laden with *agwụ* bag).[12] A ritual of restitution, to return the *agwụ* bag could finally resolve the matter.

---

12   I saw many bags that have been submitted to the *dibịa* who is the specialist in handling this crisis. It is part of the ritual that those so affected present bags containing special items as restitution to *agwụ*.

Agwụ Chi

Agwụ is positive and negative and so gets mixed up in the twists of fortune and misfortune, success and failure. *Agwụ* viewed from this perspective is similar to *chi*, for there is the good *chi* (*chi ọma*) and the bad one (*chi ọjọọ*), at the level of human diverse experiences. Both concepts are employed to explain human fate in the world.

The complexity of the idea of *chi* among the Igbo is well illustrated by the several shades of meaning that it generates. *Chi*, is variously seen as: a genius with which every human being is associated; a spiritual double given to each human being by *Chukwu* (the Supreme God) at the time of birth, which is in essence a divine part; some personalized providence that comes from *Chukwu* and reverts to him at a man's death; a guardian spirit; providence and individual fate.[13] A certain view maintains that an individual's fate is conceived not simply as an external imposition but as a deliberately chosen option. This is stated by Henderson based on his study of Onitsha area of western Igbo: "It is believed that when an individual chooses to enter the world, (*inye ụwa*) he makes a pact with a particular essential being (*chi*), selecting his length of life and his future activities; the choice so made are marked by *chi* on his hand as his *akalaka* ('marks of the hand'), or 'destiny'."[14] If this were simply so it would, however, be difficult to reconcile the many negative

---

13   Cf. G.T. Basden, *Niger Ibos*, Frank Cass & Co., London, 1966, p.37; E. Ilogu, *Christianity and Igbo Culture*, p.36; Elizabeth Isichei, *A History of the Igbo People*, Macmillan, London, 1976, p.25; Emefie Ikenga-Metuh, *God & Man in African Religion*, p. 22; Anacletus Odoemene, *The Challenges of Igbo Identity*, (Ph.D. dissertation, Hochschule für Philosophie, München, 1983), p.180.

14   Richard N. Henderson, *The King in Every Man*, New Haven, Yale University Press, 1972, p.107. Palmistry is practised by many medicine-men. During my interview with Ezenwanyi, a medicine-woman of the mermaid cult (mammy water), at Lokpanta, she demanded to read my palms. I obliged her. She told me that the spirit had just told her to do so. According to her reading, I shall be wealthy because I am the reincarnation of a great ancestor. Secondly, I am married and have children and one of them is very stubborn. For good reasons, at the end of the visit, I did not disclose to her that I am a Catholic priest.

imposing human fortunes with personal choice. Rather, such experiences as well as the positive ones are believed to have been so ordained by *chi* without any consultation of the person involved. *Chi* as a dynamic force is a guardian spirit that is supposed to intercede for a person before *Chukwu*. When a person suffers misfortune it is only because his or her *chi* is asleep. So much in human experiences are ascribed to *chi* that it has been described as "possibly one of the most complex theological concepts which both accounts for the universe, explains good and evil, tragedy and good fortune, order and conflict, character and destiny, free will and metaphysical order."[15]

Agwụ chi means, *'agwụ so madụ na chi ya abịa'* (*agwụ* accompanying a person's *chi*). Every human being that comes into the world has *chi* but *agwụ* is a spirit force whose cult is observed by those who have the calling. When the content of one's *chi* includes *agwụ*, then one's *agwụ* is *agwụ chi* . A bad *chi* and a good *agwụ* existing together is, therefore, a contradiction.

Personal Names

Personal names in Igbo traditional society usually describe the circumstances that remotely or immediately relate to the birth of children. With the strong impact of the religious world-view a good number of them are expressions of acknowledgment of and gratitude for the benevolence of the gods in granting children. *Agwụ* is one of the prominent fertility spirits and there are many names through which it is credited with marital fertility. These names ultimately point to the dynamic penetration which *agwụ* makes in the lives and activities of people;

Adaagwụ (First daughter of *agwụ*)
Agwụebuo (*agwụ* makes great)
Agwụedu (*agwụ* guides)

---

15   M.J.C. Echeruo. "A matter of Identity" (1979 Ahiajoku Lecture), Cultura Division, Ministry of Information, Culture, Youth & Sports, Owerri 1979, p.20.

Agwụike (agwụ is strength)

Agwụezuo (agwụ brings completion)

Agwụka (agwụ is supreme)

Agwụọcha (The bright *agwụ/agwụ* of good fortune)

Anyanwụagwụ (The sun/light of *agwụ*)

Ekeagwụ (The Eke market-day that is holy to *agwụ*)

Ihuọmaagwụ (Good fortune from *agwụ*)

Nwagwụ (The child born through the intervention of *agwụ*)

Nwanyiagwụ (The female child born through the intervention of *agwụ*)

Oguagwụ (The righteousness of *agwụ*)

Okoroagwụ (agwụ's son)

Osuagwụ (One that is dedicated to *agwụ* as a ritual slave)

Ugoagwụ (The eagle of *agwụ*/fortune granted by *agwụ*)

All these names describe the positive impacts of *agwụ* as a provident deity. Of course in its ambivalent nature *agwụ* is responsible for many human negative experiences. Through both positive and negative influences, *agwụ* is recognized to be very much involved in human affairs.

Initial Signs of *Agwụ* Possession

Agwụ manifests its presence in people's lives with diverse signs. At the initial stages the signs are generally of negative types. Most elderly people were conversant with traditional explanations of such symptoms. That helped them to decide when a case required the attention of the professional. It is the *dibịa* who ascertains that the intrusion of spirits other than *agwụ* is not the case since other spirits who meddle in the lives of human beings do display similar signs. He discovers this in divination. He determines the identity of the *agwụ* in question and prescribes the effective ritual remedies against its afflictions. It is well known for instance, that what the matrilineal *agwụ* eats is not always exactly what the patrilineal variety eats. The administration of medicine in such instances of *agwụ* disturbances is performed only by an expert, the *dibịa*. While ordinarily most family heads may know about the remedies to common illnesses, when indications reveal *agwụ* involvement professional services are sought.[16]

Signs of possession in Children

Agwụ can manifest in childhood or in adulthood. In the former case, the victim might be prone to excessive crying, restlessness, fever and convulsions. There might also be notable loss of weight. The *dibịa* prescribes either of two types of rites of crisis control. The first consists of the application of herbal concoctions on the body of the victim, accompanied with a simple sacrifice of fowl and a promise that the child would take up the full rite of initiation on becoming an adult. The spirit is requested to suspend further perturbations. In some places, the *dibịa* demands the erection of *ihuagwụ* (miniature shrine) as a visible sign of *ekwele m agwụ* (I say yes to *agwụ*). According to practices in Arochukwu, the rite of 'returning the *agwụ* bag' is a crisis control measure, but one that can settle finally the conflict between *agwụ* and the individual.

Another method of crisis control, which is common in Okigwe and nearby communities, consists of the rite of `*Ike akọ na uche*"(to tie intelligence and wisdom). To tie them means to control and preserve them in their symbolic forms for the child who will need them later when he becomes a *dibịa*. There is usually a sacrificial accompaniment and a pledge on behalf of the child. It was believed that unless such steps were taken the condition of the child would deteriorate and a disastrous end could result. This, it is explained accounted for so much of infant mortality in the past.

---

16   A typical reaction among the Igbo is illustrated by Okonkwo in *Things Fall Apart*, when he was informed that his daughter "Ezinma is dying." Okonkwo applied his experience to determine at once, what type of sickness that was: "It is *iba* said Okonkwo as he took his matchet and went into the bush to collect the leaves and grasses and barks of trees that went into making the medicine for *iba*". In such simple matters recourse to *dibịa* would be uncalled for. But if a minor illness persists, one would begin to suspect that *ihe a awughị okporo* (a hidden cause exists).

In Mbaise, a rite known as *anya ụta* is applied in the case of child-disturbances caused by *agwụ*. Such children would be between the ages of eight and fifteen. Anosike explained that the rite is-

> performed on children who are believed to have had great powers in their previous lives so as to set a calm pace between their previous and present lives.[17]

It is a ritual administered to a young person to sustain and enhance any tendencies he manifests towards embracing the practice of divination or herbal medicine. In other words, its purpose is to preserve the seeds of the calling that have manifested early in time. The ritual is a minor form of *ịtu anya* (opening the eyes) and in some communities it was applied to all the male children as minor initiation that sets them in the right direction and also forestalls other *agwụ* disturbances.[18]

The ritual usually takes place in *ọhịa mkpa* (the bad bush), a location that makes lasting impressions on the minds of the young people. After enduring the pains of spicy materials that are put into their eyes, they entertain the feeling of being part of a higher class in the community. As a boy, I did not undergo this rite because my parents were staunch Christians. My age mates often taunted me and claimed they could face terrifying occasions much more courageously.

Signs of Possession in Adults

The several and varied signs, symptoms and negative conditions that indicate initial possession may manifest at the biophysiological, social, economic or psychological levels. Bizarre events in individual lives are often found to indicate *agwụ* possession. Experts usually arrive to confirm the fears and predictions of relatives of a victim. Such fears are based on

---

17. Eberechukwu M. Anosike, *A Modern Healer: The life and Work of Dr. Cyril Ekenwa O. Nwogu*, Imo State University Press, Uturu (Nigeria), 1992, p.43.

18. In Isiekenesi, it was believed that "every male child... is supposed to be faced with the wrath of *Agwụ-ishi* until he goes through its rituals for a sort of cleansing." (Cf. Elias Dike Ibe, *Igbo Customs and Traditions*, Diceson Associates, Lagos, 1989, p.22).

knowledge shared by members of a community about the deities and their characteristics.

Biophysiological

The *dibịa* is likely to detect the involvement of *agwụ*, when sickness is persistent, recurrent or chronic; when there is proneness to epileptic and fainting fits; and when there are infertility, impotency and infections of venereal disease. *Agwụ* is believed to be highly pathogenic and responsible for a wide spectrum of human biological and physiological ailments.

Social

A person who is inclined to deviant behaviour or mischief is described as *onye agwụ* or *onye agwụ na awa (akpa)*. Stubbornness, aggressiveness and proneness to fighting are characteristics following *agwụ* possession. Onye *agwụ* has the tendency to quarrel with neighbours, fellow workers or business associates. One possessed by *agwụ* is irritable but he is likely to annoy and provoke others in whatever he does or says. It is said that his words burn the ears. He indulges in inappropriate and antisocial behaviour, including social withdrawal. One may still be *onye agwụ* when one is consistently the victim of injustice, assaults, false accusations and castigations. *Agwụ* makes one an unfortunate victim by manipulating all situations in one's disfavour. The female *agwụ* has a litany of pranks it could play on women. A woman under her spell loses self control and the sense of sound judgement and becomes subject to a wide range of afflictions.

> *Lọlọ* [female *agwụ*] *induces* her to be cantankerous in the home, to forget her basket after buying or selling in the market, and even to overpay for any item bargained for. The ugly aspect of it all is that the *woman* can be caught stealing and disgraced in the market when previously she was not a thief. She can become insane or childless.[19]

---

19   J. H. Orji, "*A g w ụ* Among the Ikeduru of Mbaitoli/Ikeduru Local Government Area," Thesis presented for a B.A. at the University of Nigeria, Nsukka p.24.

Unusual Occurrences

Bizarre occurrences generally are interpreted as *agwu* instruments of coercion. Every important *dibịa* could recount some odd experiences in the realization of his vocation. Take for instance, the account of Nwogu Madugba who fell fourteen times while climbing trees, but who unlike his father, who had an exact record, sustained no deforming injuries. Nwogu also had experiences of the attack of queer diseases that continued to disturb him for many years until he initiated as a *dibịa*.[20]

Another informant, Chief Jona Olo, who had abandoned Christianity to become a *dibịa*, and who at the time I interviewed him had once more reverted to Christianity explained his action as reaction to shocking events in his family. Before the events, Chief Jona was a member of the African Church of Christ (ACC.) and a polygamist, for the practice is allowed in this church. He had two wives and was blessed with many children. During the three-year Nigeria/Biafra war, fifteen of his children died from malnutrition. In a single day alone five died. His son who was a Captain in the Biafran army died four months before the end of the war. The experiences left him with a crushing emotional shock that threw doubt on the almighty powers of his Christian God, whom he had accepted as benefactor and saviour.

Jona failed to attribute the cause of the death of his children to malnutrition no matter how certain that seemed because other families around him who were also subject to the same deprivations did not have experiences as drastic as his. When he sought further clarification from fortune tellers the revelations were frightening. He was informed he would lose the remaining members of his family if he continued to try the power of *agwu* of his maternal family. He was·blamed for having failed to recognize all along the messages embodied in the death of his children. Jona accepted initiation and practised as *dibịa* for twenty years before coming back to the Church. He did so after some members of the Prophet-Healing-Church had visited him

---

20   Nwogu Madugba, Oral interview.

while he was seriously sick in hospital and predicted that he would never recover unless he renounced the *agwụ* cult and returned to the church. His *ụlọ agwụ* (*agwụ* house) where he carried out consultations for his work as *dibịa*, is still standing although looking desolate. His return to Christianity notwithstanding, Jona still firmly maintains that he is a *dibịa*. He believes that *dibịa* initiation imparted on him a character that is permanent."[21]

Another informant recounted a weird incident which took place in a town near Owerri in 1973 and which had been generally believed to have been the result of *agwụ* possession. A man who for years had remained heedless to invitations from *agwụ* was on a fateful afternoon driven into some fit of insanity as a result of which he mutilated himself by cutting off his genitals. The piece of penis was successfully reattached after the man himself had raised an alarm and was rushed to the hospital. After this affliction, he became convinced of his possessed condition and promptly submitted to the rites of initiation. There is no limit to the odd designs which *agwụ* could bring about.

Economic

Economic disasters are signs of possession. *Agwụ* strikes with the economic disease known as *aka ọkụ* or *akpata atụfuo* (inability to save money or money wasting). The spirit induces spendthriftiness or causes mysterious disappearance of money, domestic animals and other belongings. There are generally disappointments and frustrations in the person's occupation or trade. Harvests are poor and to describe the situation, the Igbo say: *'agwụ gara ya n'ọrụ'*. Northcote Thomas' study provides more information on the economic disasters which are believed to be caused by *agwụ*:

> I was definitely informed that this *Agụ* [*agwụ*] spoils yams, and when nothing will divert him from this occupation, the owner becomes a doctor, hence *agu* is an *alose [alụsị]*; even a woman may become a doctor in these circumstances.[22]

---

21 . Jona Olo, Oral interview .

22 . Northcote W. Thomas, *Law and Custom of the Ibo of the Awka Neighbourhood S. Nigeria*, p.39.

In trading, one possessed by *agwu* records very poor sales, the goods are often stolen or simply get missing. An informant has thus recounted his experience of *agwu* interference in his baking business:

> At every attempt to produce bread something went wrong. When the bread did not get burnt in the oven, even at the lowest of baking temperature conditions, it quickly swelled and then shrivelled into small hard balls, which no one cared to buy.[23]

Psychological

Indications of possession at this level include experiences of nightmares especially ones where the person's life is exposed to grave dangers. To be attacked or pursued in the dream by dogs and to get close to drowning are well known signs of possession. These are more easily confirmed as valid signs when such dreams keep repeating. Other signs of possession include, somnambulation, soliloquizing, endless murmuring, lack of control in talking. It is said that *'agwu na-akpafu mmadu uka n'onu '*.[24] There may be muddling of the mind, hallucinations, and delusion. It is said, *onye agwu na-akpa bu onye anya na-edoghi edo'* (one possessed by *agwu* does not perceive or understand correctly).

The tendency to steal, fight, rape or attempt suicide is a well known symptom of *agwu*. Most times, the possessed is unaware of the actions he performs. Whether he is aware or not it is held that *agwu edufuole ya* (*agwu* has deceived or misled him). *Onye agwu* shows in his interactions with others much emotional and psychological disorders. Mental instability and insanity (*ara agwu*) are the last plagues when a victim cannot be turned off the path of intransigence, to submit to initiation.

---

23. Aja Kalu, Oral interview.
24. It is strongly believed that if one stealthily commits a crime, *agwu* could induce one sometime, somewhere, to confess it and this is referred to as *agwu ikpafu madu uka n'onu*. Women thus confess their infidelities to their husbands and thieves to the hearing of neighbours.

Initial Control Rituals in the case of *Agwụ* Possession

The expert knowledge of the diviner is required to analyze each condition of possession. It is believed that while a person remains inattentive to the presence of *agwụ* the negative conditions worsen. In some cases the possessed would not be required to go the full length in initiation ceremony. Those who for reasons of age or lack of resources could not be initiated as soon as symptoms of possession manifest are expected to apply some control rituals whose purpose is to set a person temporarily on a harmonious relationship with *agwụ*, so that *agwụ* could suspend its negative influences.

A control ritual is *ikwenkwụ agwụ* or *ekwele m ime agwụ*. It is a simple rite by which the individual expresses his consent to that proposal for which possession was intended and so is willing to be initiated into *agwụ* cult. *Agwụ* itself is requested to suspend its affliction for the period which is considered sufficient for the individual to be prepared for initiation.

The rite of giving consent is contractual in nature. It states the obligations and rites of both *agwụ* and the human victim. The terms are clearly pronounced by the officiating *dibịa* as he inserts pegs of the ritual plants in their specific places at the shrine, as this version of the formula shows;

Agwụ iwe gị jụrụ
Ma ugbu a o dolu m anya [ihe] wụ uche gị.
Ego adịghị m n'aka,
Nye aka kpata ego eji eme nkea.
Site taa ruo afọ atọ aga m eme dịka i si choo.
Ala, ndichie bụrụ nụ ndi aka ebe.

Agwụ abate your rage.
And now I am fully aware of your will towards me.
I have no money to undergo an ordination,
Help me to procure the fund needed for this.
(Before three years are over) I shall do what you demand
Earth goddess, ancestors, be witnesses.[25]

Following this agreement, or understanding, *agwụ* is not only bound to desist from actions that have negative effects, it is also expected to help positively by promoting the economic and social well-being of the individual. If *agwụ* fails to do so at the end of the period and the aspirant has not saved enough money for the initiation ceremony, *agwụ* is blamed for failing to bring prosperity. A common expectation in Igbo religion is that deities should assist their devotees in their pursuit of material well-being so that the devotees would have the resources to worship them.

The rite of giving consent does not always take place at the shrine. Certain indications of possession call for rites at or close to the site where the signs manifest. An informant, Aforibe, from Nkoto Ihube explained that sacrifices had to be offered at the stream where, in his dream, he narrowly escaped being caught by spirits. The spirits had pursued him and he heard them shouting, "catch him, catch him, he has returned". Aforibe's father who was a *dibịa* at once deciphered the dream to be a sign of *agwụ*. He prepared a tray with fresh palm leaves *(Igboaja)* and put in it, four coins, white chalk, yellow chalk, parts of a slaughtered chicken, and placed the tray beside the stream.

The malign influences of *agwụ* directed at a home is a form of possession which generates belligerency and unruly temperaments in its members. This was the popular way to explain frequent dissension in the family. It is said that *agwụ ọjọọ ebikwutele ha* (the bad *agwụ* has moved in with them). The

---

25. Cf. J. H. Orji, *Agwụ Among the Ikeduru of Mbaitoli/Ikeduru Local Government Area*, p.28. There are slight modifications of the orthography of the Igbo text as well as the English translation of the original text, for the purpose of easier reading.

dibịa is expected to drive away the negative force from the house and to replace it with a positive one. The exorcism consists in cleansing the house by sweeping it, and the dirt collected there, which symbolize *agwụ ọjọọ,* is carried far away from the house by the *dibịa.* The family is assured that it has an *agwụ* tradition and the member whose dereliction has provoked *agwụ's* temper, in view of this rite of consent, would begin to prepare for the appropriate rite of initiation.

As a result of its exceedingly perforative effects on human life and activities, reflections on *agwụ* went beyond simply affirming its existence as one of the creatures of *Chukwu.* Hence, myths and stories of *agwụ* constitute a large part of the corpus of Igbo religious myths. The myths and beliefs have also found generous expressions in art and symbols. We shall in the next chapter briefly examine the nature of these expressions.

Chapter 3

Art And Symbol In *Agwụ* Cult

Art in *Agwụ* 'cult Practices

Anthropomorphism is a feature of Igbo religious art. It shows gods who have human shapes and observe sociocultural behaviour patterns as men do. The question of religious art involves what Tillich has called the 'ultimate concern', and no matter how much it lacks in grandeur, it is still characterized by a mysterious aspect.[1] Beattie explains the function of art in archaic societies to mean that;

> most such art is a way of expressing, in sensory form and usually in an idiom comprehensible to the people for whom it is made, concepts, attitudes and values which are held in particular regard in a given culture.[2]

Whether the choice of artistic theme are divine figures, images of key values in the religious tradition or some key doctrines of faith, the purpose is to present them in a way that they could be intellectually and emotionally appreciated.

Eliade has discussed the symbolic value of art in ancient societies pointing out the belief in divine involvement in its production. Religious art according to him,

> translated religious experience and a metaphysical conception of the world and of human existence into a concrete, representational form. This translation was not considered wholly the work of man: the divinity also participated by revealing himself to man and allowing himself to be perceived in form or figure. Every religious expression in art represents therefore, an encounter between man and the divine. Such encounters may be, on the one hand, a personal religious experience, or

---

1   Paul Tillich, "Culture as Expression of Ultimate Concern." In Edward Cell (editor), *Religion and Contemporary Western Culture*, Nashville Abingdon, New York, 1967, p.89.

2   John Beattie, *Other Cultures*, Routledge & Kegan Paul, London, 1964, 205.

on the other, a religious perception of the world, the discovery that the
world is a divine work, the creation of gods.[3]
This perception is present in Igbo religious culture. Artistic
production is seen as an enterprise involving the divine, for
agwụ in traditional departmentalization of gods and spirits is the
patron of artistic works. The artist *(omenka/omeọka)* in the
execution of a particular work, either carving objects on wood or
moulding them on clay, is believed to be under the guidance of
this spirit. His very professional calling is an election by the
spirit who endows him with knowledge of the images of the
divine beings and their characteristics. However, the artist is not
a passive collaborator. His works bear the imprint of his
measure of imaginativeness, intelligence, and experience.
The sacred quality attributed to artistic work is evident in the
practice of situating its production within some sacred milieu or
environment, such as the groove in the heart of a forest. In some
cases, a work place in the home is used and usually such a place
is set apart with taboos.[4]
Since art work of all types fall primarily within the sphere of
agwụ superintendence, artistic and symbolic representations of
objects of *agwụ* cult practices are profuse. The several
illustrations of *agwụ* have concentrated on the questions relating
to its gender, social relations and activities. And generally, such
preoccupations have dictated the styles and forms in the tradition
of African religious art. This mutual interdependence, of the

---

3   Mircea Eliade, *Symbolism, the Sacred, the Arts*, Crossroad, New York,
1986, p.55.

4   For details of the function of taboos in ordering human beings, objects and
space, see, J.C.U. Aguwa, "Taboos and Purification of Ritual Pollutions in
Igbo Traditional Society: Analysis and Symbolisms", *Anthropos* 88
(1993):539-546. Edogo, in *Arrow of God*, when carving masks, "he could
not do it in the home under the profane gaze of women and children but had
to retire to the spirit-house built for such work at a secluded corner of the
Nkwo market place where no one who had not been initiated into the secret
of Masks would dare to approach." It is indicated that this house provided
inspiration for the carver: "Apart from the need for secrecy, Edogo had
always found the atmosphere of this hut right for carving masks. All around
him were older masks and other regalia of ancestral spirits, some of them
older than even his father. They produce a certain ambience which gave
power and cunning to his fingers." (Chinua Achebe, *Arrow of God*, London,
Heinemann, p.51.)

natural and the supernatural worlds, has led Schillebeeckx to conclude that:

> every religious statement about the holy is in fact a statement about man and his world, but in the sense that every religious statement about man and the world is in reality also a statement about the holy, about God.[5]

This is also upheld in the belief in the mutual collaboration of the human intellect and divine revelation in the creation of religious art.

The spread of artistic representations of *agwụ* do not divide strictly along subcultural lines, for divergent views are held among people even in the same locality. The most common sculptural representation of *agwụ* in statues of wood or clay is of a household- a family of the male (*oke agwụ*), the wife (*nwunye agwụ*), their son (*okoro agwụ*) and their daughter (*agboghọ agwụ*). Agwụ ancestry (*ọkpụ agwụ* or *obi agwụ*) is represented symbolically with an encased bundle of feathers and four sticks. *Obi agwụ* is the 'heart' of the reality, the quintessence, the affirmation that provides the existential logic for the entire household. The lower members of the household include statuettes of, *osuagwụ* (ritual slave) and *ohu agwụ* (slave of *agwụ*). Whether carved on wood or made with clay, the members of the household are distinguished in their proper gender characteristics.

The artistic style which is employed to capture the mysterious and transcendental nature of *agwụ* is the multi-headed representation. Usually, four heads sharing a frame and facing the opposite directions is the common style. The dominant interpretation found in the history of religions is that "many headedness signifies that a god is capable of looking in different directions at the same time, that he is all-seeing and consequently omniscient."[6] *Agwụ* is an enigma and a mystery. The four-headed *agwụ* image also points to the supervision which *agwụ* exercises over the Igbo four-day week, namely *Eke, Orie, Afọ,*

5 Edward Schillebeeckx, Christ: *The Christian Experience in the Modern World,* SCM Press, London, 1982, p.776.
6 Mircea Eliade, *Symbolism, the Sacred, the Arts,* p.3.

and *Nkwọ*. This four-day period represents the totality of cosmic time.

The prevailing view in some parts of Igboland affirming the femininity of *agwụ* is copiously expressed in art. In such places as Owerri and Ngwa where the view is strongly held, the spirit is sculpturally represented as a single female. In Ngwa area particularly, a prominent statue highlighting female physical characteristics is usually chosen, with smaller statues of female attendants. In Emekuku community the statue is placed at the shrine between two attendants called *nyei agwụisi* and *ọgazị agwụisi*. To these divine images, cult members pour laudatory verses extolling *agwụ* as embodying maximally those properties belonging to the essence of womanhood. That *agwụ* is female, an informant explained, is evident in the effect which it produces, for as a man becomes dazed and loses his head and sanity over love for a woman, so is one affected when one is possessed by *agwụ*. In Ngwa area the patronage of *agwụ* of human fertility is highly acknowledged. It reached to the point that cases of infertility and the occurrences of venereal diseases are attribuied to the scourge of *agwụ* on erring or stubborn devotees.[7] When one considers that the Igbo name for venereal disease is *nsị nwanyị* (woman poison), to identify *agwụ* as source of it is to affirm *agwụ* dominant femininity. How this belief affected attitude to and treatment of the disease in the past can easily be imagined.

Symbols in *Agwụ* Cult Practices

Religion or religious cult is exercised through rituals or systems of symbolic actions by which. the religious reality is made present to the senses. Flourishing religious thoughts and perspectives, which are cosmocentric, anthropocentric and anthropomorphic, enhance the development of a wide variety of artistic representations, as we have seen. There are also varieties

---

7   Nwogu Madugba, oral interview. He is a *dibịa* and the leader of the *dibịa* league in his locality. The group of people who were present during the interview shared the view which was firmly held by Madugba.

of objects with which the reality and the object of worship are expressed and represented. These objects may be natural, phylomorphic or theriomorphic. The dependence of a symbol on an existing religious reality is a fundamental presumption in the creation of religious symbols. Eliade points out that it has been a condition from the earliest practices of religious symbolization.

> From the beginning of archaic cultures, a hierophany is simultaneously an ontophany, the manifestation of the sacred is equivalent to an unveiling of Being and vice versa. It follows that archaic religious symbolism is dependent upon an ontology. From a particular point of view, the symbol itself may be considered as a language which, although conceptual is nevertheless capable of expressing a coherent thought on existence and on the world.[8]

On the evaluation of the attitude to symbols by people of Southern Nigeria, Talbot remarked :

> With very few exceptions the deities are represented by symbols, before which sacrifices are offered and all prayers made. Save perhaps in a few cases among the ignorant, these are never thought to be gods themselves, but only as affording a convenient means of concentrating the attention and providing a point of worship. [9]

As in the case of religious art, in most instances of establishing religious symbols, the human actor is taken to be a collaborator of the deity. In studying the application of symbols in *agwụ* cult we shall see how much this is true. We shall also see the nature of relationships between the symbols and the realities.

Life Symbols

The symbols with which the existence and vitality of *agwụ* are primarily affirmed do not have intrinsic or extrinsic or causal relations to the subjects. In the cultural area where such symbols are found, they represent some conventional tradition in the process of religious symbolization. While responding to our inquiry on how to establish that *agwụ* really exists, an informant who is an *agwụ* specialist and well-versed in the cult brought out

---

8 Murcea Eliade, *Symbolism, the Sacred, the Arts*, p.3.
9 P. Amaury Talbot, *The Peoples of Southern Nigeria*, Frank Cass & Co., London, 1969, pp.19-20.

two sticks of unequal sizes and explained: This one (holding
out the longer stick) is *ukwu agwu* (the legs of *agwu*).
Whatever has legs exists. This other, is *oṇịra akụ* and it is the
mouth through which *agwụ* consumes sacrifice. It eats, and
therefore it is alive.[10] The explanation has taken into account
the fundamental question of existence of *agwụ*, and goes to
assert the pre-existence of a reality over its symbols, which
means that symbols represent realities whose existence they
presuppose. *Obi agwụ* (the heart of *agwụ*) represented with a
bundle of feathers encasing four sticks belongs to this category
of symbols.

Anthroposocial Symbols
Following the anthroposocial scheme in which the world of the
spirits is revealed to men, whatever is socially valued is often an
essential constituent of revelation. Igbo vital social symbols -
ofọ, ogu, ikenga - are also key symbols in the *agwụ* cult. *Ofọ* is
"a male symbol that primarily represents ancestral power and
authority and the key values of truth and justice."[11] It is taken
from the branch of the *ofọ* tree and later consecrated for ritual
and social purposes. Authority, truth and justice are values
believed to be fundamental to the building-up and ordering of the
human society and since the world of the spirits is conceived as
similar to that of men, these values are found also in the former.
Hence, *ofọ* is a reality of the world of the spirits.The priest of
the *agwụ* cult, the diviner and the physician must officially be
handed the *ofọ agwụ* which is symbol of authority in cult
matters.

Ofọ is the basis of the relationship which *agwụ* has with
other deities and spirits, whose 'spokesman' it is. Human beings
confidently enter into relationships of a *quid pro quo* nature,
armed with the faith that the *ofọ* spirit force kills defaulters, men
and gods alike. It is because *agwụ* is believed to be capable of

10 Onyeakobusi Uwakwe, Oral interview.
11 C.I. Ejizu, "The Taxonomy, Provenance and Functions of *ofọ*, A Dominant
Igbo Ritual and Political Symbol", *Anthropos* 82(1987): 547-467.

abiding by the ethic of reciprocal response, at least to some degree under the pressure of *ofọ* that rituals carried out by human beings are believed to be capable of producing results. What guarantees the promises of men and gods is the force of *ofọ*, who is the ruthless avenger against those who perpetrate dishonesty, injustice and deceit.

A twin virtue of *ofọ* is *ogu*. It stands for righteousness, a virtue that should characterize the actions of men and gods alike. Interaction among human beings and with gods, or interaction among the gods themselves is monitored by *ogu*, that discovers actions which are unrighteous, unjust, condemnable and sure to bring harm to the performer. It is a vital ethical force that demands only those actions which are approvable. In entering into a relationship with *agwụ*, the person does so with *ogu* and expects that *agwụ* would do the same. A person considers a contract made with *agwụ* no longer binding on him, if he discovers that *agwụ* has reneged on the terms of the agreement. In that case, the person is said to have *ofọ na ogu* (justice and righteousness) on his side before which the powers of *agwụ* or any other deity, no matter how strong, would crumble in defeat.

With *ofọ and ogu* as guarantors, agreements are made and honoured. Neither a human being nor a god could escape the retributive power of *ogu*, for it is that positive power within each person, whose suppression has effects of bringing a person to self-contradiction, diminishment and destruction. *Ogu* provides the norms for actions for a harmonious relationship of two parties. The adoption of the symbols of *ofọ* and *ogu* in the *agwụ* ritual cult must have been considered even more significant in view of needed measures to combat *agwụ* characteristic capriciousness and ambivalence.

Ikenga agwụ (ikenga or *ike m ji aga* - the power I move with, or *ike m gaa* - let my force and strength advance), represents that great command which *agwụ* exercises over cosmic force and through which it brings success to the possessor of the symbol object. *Ikenga* is a vital socio-religious symbol of power and strength. It is the spiritual force for success and achievement. To get access to this spirit force, a man's right hand, the physical symbol of his strength and resolve to succeed is ritualized and thus brought into communication with cosmic force. The carved *ikenga* ritual object forms are generally characterized by a pair of up-thrusting ram-like horns to depict, according to Ejizu, the "stubborn determination observed to be a natural characteristic of ram and said to belong at least in some analogical way to *Ikenga* spirit force."[12]

There are several areas of human life and activities that are assigned to the supervision of *agwụ*. Success and excellence in these areas require that the deity commands a massive range of cosmic force, that is, that *agwụ* should control a dynamic and powerful *ikenga*. It is explained that,

> before a particular *agwụ* is considered due to get an *Ikenga object*, it should have distinguished itself as a favourite ally and generator of success for the owner. Thus, with the consecration of this special class of *Ikenga symbol* for the patron deity (*agwụ*), the professional now enjoys the fullest support of the spirit-force of achievement in his practice.[13]

Plant Symbols

Plant hierophany, that is, the sacred expressed in plant has wide recognition in Igbo religious culture.[14] Plants used in the erection and building of shrines, and those recognized as sacred because of their religious significance have popular hierophanic value. Trees or plants are sacred, essentially, for the sacred reality they represent. As Eliade explains,

> ... no tree or plant is ever sacred simply as a tree or plant; they become so because they share in a transcendental reality, they become so

---

12 Christopher I. Ejizu, *Ritual Enactment of Achievement: Ikenga Symbol in Igboland*, PAIDEUMA 37 (1991) p.234.

13 *Ibid.*, p.240.

14 B.N. Okigbo has identified 29 sacred plants in the Igbo environment. Cf."Plants and Food in Igbo Culture" (1980 Ahiajoku Lecture), Culture Division, Ministry of Information, Culture Youth and Sports, Owerri, 1980, pp.33-4.

because they signify that transcendent reality. By being consecrated, the individual 'profane' plant species is transubstantiated....[15]

Since "to the primitive mind, nature and symbol were inseparable,"[16] the literalist attitude prevailed in describing the mysterious relationship resulting from the sacredness of such plants or trees. Idowu's observation is that "such a tree as spirits inhabit becomes their emblem, at the foot of it offerings are made to them and people make ejaculatory prayers as they pass by."[17]

Ogirisi (Newbouldia Laevis) is a very important ritual plant in *agwụ* cult. It features more regularly at the shrine than any other plant. It had become so popular in *agwụ* rituals that it fell victim of the literalist tendency and began to be used synonymously with *agwụ*. Hence, *ogirisi* is also known as *agwụ ụmụnne* or simply *ụmụnne* (*agwụ* of the maternal home).

Ogirisi and two other popular ritual plants namely, *abọsị* (camwood/Baphis Nitida) and *ọha* (Pterocarpus Soyauxii), used in erecting *agwụ* shrines have such qualities that may have suggested their suitability for religious evaluation. All of these plants have very high survival ability and do not shed their leaves in the dry season. Therefore, as regards ritual option, they have much advantage since most other plants which are seasonal shed leaves in the dry season. When employed in the erection of the shrine, their evergreen leaves sustain perennially, the living image of the shrine. The shrine which, following popular conceptions, is where the deity lives, must be seen always to radiate life and power. Life and power constitute the essence of divinity. A withered shrine reflects the crisis of lost essence.

Ogirisi and *abọsị* are used for other purposes such as in setting land or farm boundaries. Their suitability derive from their emblematic relation to the deity. Hence they serve as authentic and irrefutable witnesses against which no disputation would be admitted, and all lies considered sacrilegious. The sap

---

15 Mircea Eliade, *Symbolism, the Sacred, the Arts*, p.268.

16 *Ibid.* p.268.

17 E.B. Idowu, *African Traditional Religion: A Definition*, SCM Press, London, 1973, p.177.

of both plants is non-toxic and so the branchlets are used as chewing stick; the leaves, particularly of *ogirisi*, are preferred for packaging.

Particular tree species become hierophanies if they are located at certain environments. *Akpʉ* (Silk cotton/Ceiba Pentandra) and *ǫjị̈* (*Iroko*/Chlorophora Excelsa) are such trees that depict values for *agwʉ* when they germinate and grow in the family compound, instead of in the forest. The occurrence is, in some places, interpreted as sign of vocation (see Appendix 2).

These two trees grow to enormous sizes and as they stand in the family compound they pose possible threat to life and houses. The overbearing and compelling divine will that is depicted in their massive sizes intensifies their symbolic value. Then the danger they pose easily fades from the minds of those who live in the vicinity. The awe for their sacred nature and the great symbolism of their presence dispel any fears of the physical danger they could bring about.

Accounts of informants point to disastrous repercussions that could follow should such trees be mishandled by pruning or by being cut down.[18] This is because of the mystical entanglement of the tree and the life of the family in which it has appeared. It is believed that if it is pruned a family member would be afflicted with a deforming injury, and if cut down the corresponding consequence is death (see Appendix 2). There is a sympathetic touch about the relationship such that the tree is said to react to the natural tragedies that occur in the family, such as withering a branch when a member of the family dies.[19]

Akpu, which provides soft wood is called *akpʉ ori mgbǫ* (*akpʉ* that swallows bullets). The trees, *akpʉ* and *ǫjị̈*, as a result

---

[18]   Obiora Nwabude very firmly connected his father's death to the cutting of the *akpʉ* that germinated in their compound. Later the stump revived and grew into a very big tree.

[19]   Obiora Nwabude's experience was that when one of his brothers died, his *akpʉ* let one of its three branches wither. It is remarkable that this tree had three branches representing Obiora and his two brothers. But the tree is there particularly for him. He recounts how the spirit of this tree had been his guardian especially in the most trying times of his life.(Cf. Appendix 2)

of their firmness, massiveness and elegance, are highly polymetaphoric. Their top are not easily accessible to men and become therefore, most secure place for birds to rest and make their nests. For human beings the trees supply expansive shade. They provide also exceptionally favoured wood for furniture and building and they are therefore, economically very valuable. But standing in the compound, they are mysteriously intertwined with life's rhythm and they are intensively expressive of the imposing transcendental reality. They are held as sacred through the taboos which are observed on their behalf. They signify the presence of *agwu* in a family.

Theriomorphic Symbols of Agwu

Representation of *agwu* in animal shapes is not usual but certain animals chosen for their particular characteristics are used in the symbolic codification of *agwu* transcendental qualities. Such qualities include foresightedness, perceptivity and omniscience. They are sculpturally expressed with the forms of the animals, which still are poor representations for qualities which could be maximally attributed to *agwu*. In their natural state however, these animals do not attract any worship or special respect for contributing to the symbolic expression of *agwu*.

Agwu is credited with tremendous foresightedness. This is represented with the carved image of *ulili* (squirrel), hence *ulili agwu*.[20] When *ulili* runs along the path, it intermittently halts and stands on its hind legs, raises up the forelegs and examines them in search of traces of danger that could lie ahead. *Ulili* is able to read the signs left on its path and to undertake a prognosis. The traditional mind has evaluated this habitual quest for warnings and foreknowledge in their analogical relation to the prevision characteristic of *agwu*. *Ulili agwu* is an important cult furniture and must be present for the empowerment of medicines intended to bring about the specific effects. The *dibia* in the exercise of his calling as diviner or physician finds *ulili agwu* a very indispensable equipment.

---

20 *Ulili* is a northern Igbo word.

Udele (the vulture) is also adopted in the symbolic scheme to represent the highly perceptive ability of *agwụ*. The vulture seems quite apt given its extraordinary power to sense carcasses even when such are quite far away. The exaggerated dimension to which myths and folklore have celebrated this power in the vulture makes its choice for the symbolic representation of an analogous *agwụ* property quite appropriate. Far more than other deities *agwụ* detects the most hidden misdemeanor. The *dibịa* who possesses a carved vulture (*udele agwụ*) is assisted by the deity to exercise a great power of perception of events and situations. He needs not be physically present to be aware of the facts of certain matters and events.

Mbe (the tortoise) is another theriomorphic symbol of the cult, and apparently a very indispensable one. In traditional folktales, the tortoise is the trickster, the most intelligent and crafty of all animals (*mbe bụ onye amamihe, onye oke akọ, onye aghụghọ*). The tortoise has therefore, been chosen in the symbolization of the omniscient attribute of *agwụ*, reckoned as the most intelligent and shrewd of divine beings for which reason it is their spokesperson. *Agwụ* is the spirit of divination, in which sphere it manifests unlimited knowledge on all things. The tortoise is a fitting symbol of this ever transcending divine attribute.

Rather than a sculptural representation, a real shell of the tortoise is used. This is understandable, given that it is durable and available and in its representative status more intensively eloquent and evocative. During divination, the diviner beats the shell to summon the spirits.

The dynamic symbolic value of *mbe is* also realized in those rituals where an actual tortoise is used, as in the traditional rite of inoculation *(igbusi ahụ),* or in the rite of *itụ anya* during initiation of the *dibịa*. In the preparation of certain antidotes, the flesh of the tortoise is an essential ingredient. It is attributed with the ability to neutralize the power of certain poisons and the Igbo therefore say *mbe dị nwayọọ* (the tortoise is gentle). Again, magical charms or substances which enable one to disappear or become invisible are prepared among other things, with the flesh of the tortoise for it is also said that *mbe bu enwo* (the tortoise is illusion).

The dog *(nkita)* is another important source of the symbolisms in the *agwu* cult. The carved image of the dog is an essential article of *agwu* cult paraphernalia. In fact, the dog features very much in the rites of the cult, not only for sacrifices but also as the animal that could be dedicated to *agwu*. The carved dog which the *dibia* acquires and calls *oga ozi agwu* (the messenger of *agwu*) provides him access to vital *agwu* perfections of swiftness and perceptivity.

Some qualities of the dog may have justified its association with *agwu*. It has natural swiftness and it has a keen perceptive power which enables it to smell out 'bad medicine' where they might be hidden. In the dark, dogs are able to 'see' not only men but also spirits. Those dogs that have 'four eyes' *(nkita anya ano)* are greatly valued in rituals for they all the more embody these qualities.[21] Another important point on which the ritual evaluation of the dog is based, is that like human beings, the dog could suffer madness, a malady which is believed to be caused by *agwu*. In fact, one of the symptoms of *agwu* possession is the recurring encounter with dogs in dreams. The *dibia* in his work is more proficient when he has the carved dog *(nkita agwu)* for he is then able to gain entrance into the world of perfection and power behind this symbol. Usually the *dibia* would acquire this symbol only at the behest of *agwu* itself and in some localities, it is a sign that *agwu* is favourably disposed towards the devotee when it orders him to do so.

---

[21] *Nkita anya ano* (the dog of four eyes) refers to dogs that have a colour shading just above their eyes. These shadings are literally counted ⸴ the doubles of the real eyes. They symbolize the more potent mysticaᵢ eyes with which the dog sees spiritual beings and also sees in the dark.

Pictures

Obi agwụ: Symbol of agwụ ancestry

Agwụ symbols from Nkoto Ihube, Okigwe

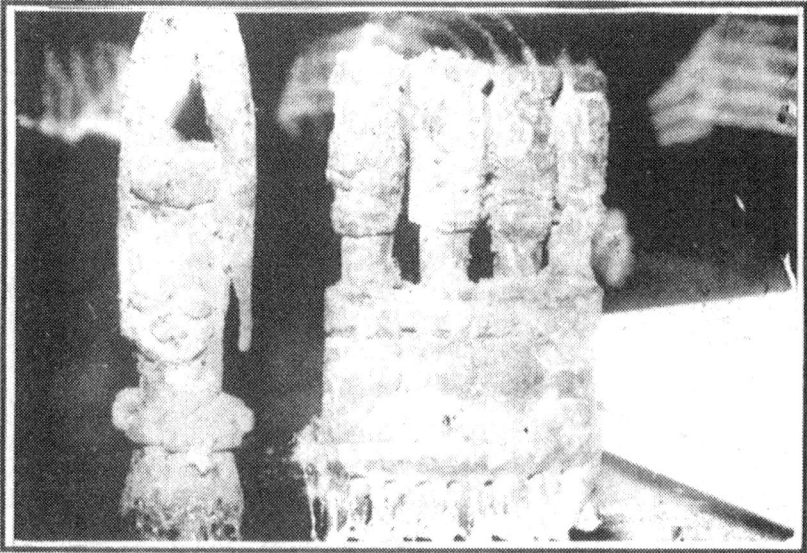

Representations of agwụ from Ekwereazu Mbaise: (1)as a single personality (2) as multi-headed god.

Ikenga agwụ (Courtesy of Odinani Museum, Nri).

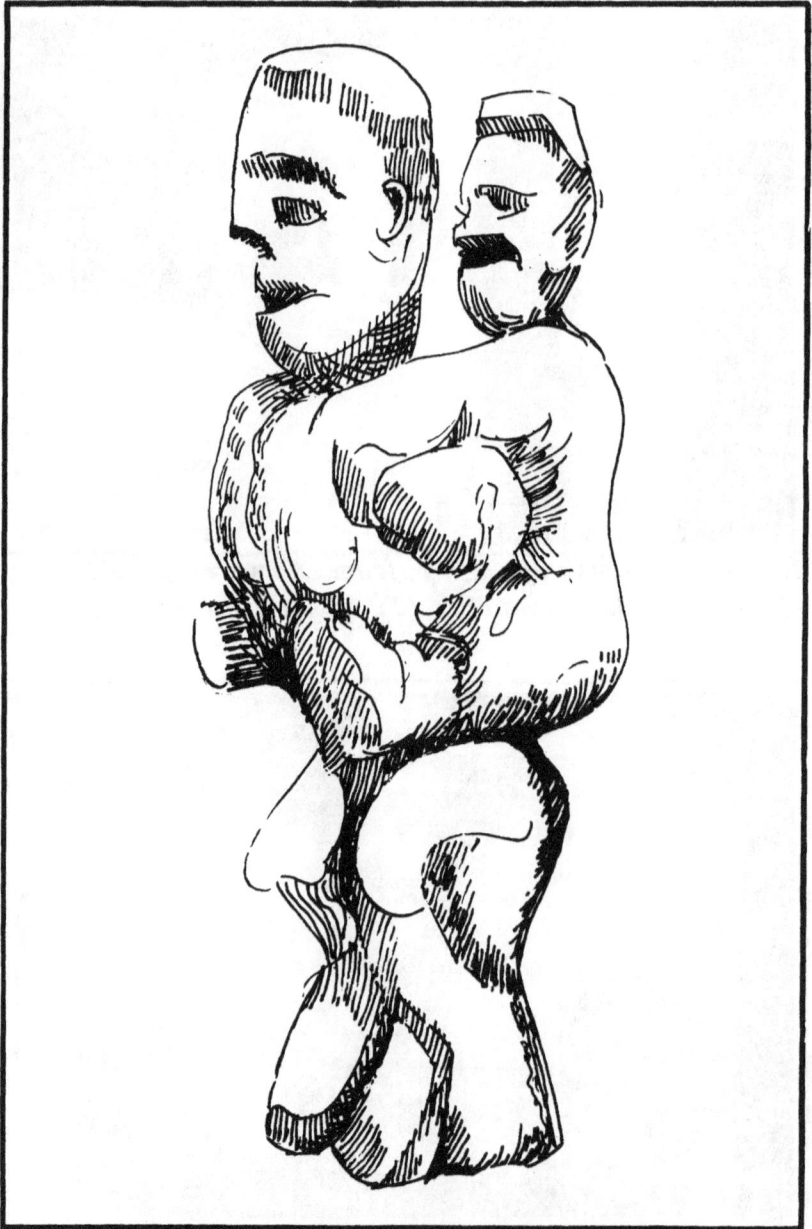

Inyom na nwata agwụ (Mother and Child)

Chapter 4

The Rites Of *Dibịa* Initiation

Dibịahood is a vocation. *Agwụ* chooses and calls men and women to its service and for special privileges. The Igbo therefore say, *agwụ na-awa awa*.[1] Some people are called to the priesthood of the cult, others summoned to be diviners or physicians. But in most cases, the one and the same person performs the three functions. In that case, the treatment of a disease for instance, may require the same person to do the diagnoses, give medication and officiate at the healing rituals.

Initiation of the *dibịa* exposes the work of healing or divination which he does, to powerful spiritual influence. The *dibịa does* not, therefore, rely only on his knowledge of the local pharmacopoeia and their applications. Based on initiation, distinction is made between a *dibịa* and another specialist of medicinal herbs who has not undergone initiation. The latter relies absolutely on his knowledge or talent and does not have the benefit of power and inspirations from the patron deity. The popular belief as stated by Ikenga-Metuh is that,

> ... medicine prepared by a *dibịa is* more powerful not only because he is an expert but because he is in possession of *agwụnsị,* a deity for medicine, whom he can invoke to give power to his medicine. So *ogwụ* is not just herbs; it must be charged with spiritual power by the use of rites, spells and invocations.[2]

The same is true of divination. By its very nature, it remains merely human effort fraught with interpretative errors until the practitioner has undergone the ritual process that opens up to him the necessary riches of spiritual power and inspirations. A good

---

[1] Generally, however, all categories of priests and other religious specialists claim the divine initiative in their callings. Such claims serve to authenticate their practice and enhance their acceptability by the public.

[2] Emefie Ikenga-Metuh, *God & Man in African Religion,* p.97.

knowledge of the hermeneutical techniques is an asset in divination but only when it has spiritual support through initiation.

Higher grades of *dibia* include those known as the *eze dibia* (chief dibia) and the *dibia iku mmuo* (necromancer). Those in these groups undergo more complicated and expensive initiations. They practise divination through which the spirit of a dead person is called up and questioned about such matters as the cause of his death or his opinion on a particular issue of family interest. In parts of southern Igboland, in more distant past, an ordinary *dibia* required the minimum of twenty years experience to initiate as a necromancer. In the present times, five years of practice are considered sufficient. Many people these days, more than in the past, can easily amass the resources needed for the expensive initiation. It is clear that economic progress has had great impact on religious observances.

The *dibia is* a man possessed by *agwu*. Describing possession John Beattie said;

> We have spirit possession when a person assumes a state of apparent auto-hypnosis or dissociation, and his behaviour which is not that of his ordinary self, is understood to be due to control by some spiritual agent normally outside himself.[3]

There are two phases in *agwu* possession, the pre-initiation and the post-initiation. While both phases manifest conditions resulting from the intervention of the spiritual agent, the characteristics are drastically different. We have already examined the negative effects that constitute possession in a pre-initiation phase. This situation changes in the second instance. After initiation the *dibia begins* to experience positive supernatural influences in his life and work.

Ideas of Initiation

Dibia initiation has various names in the many subcultural groups in Igboland. It is *isa agwu* (acquiring knowledge about *agwu*); *irulilu agwu* (fastening *agwu* to a spot); *igwo agwu* (obtaining healing for *agwu* afflictions); *ime agwu* (celebrating

---

3   John Beattie, *Other Cultures*, p.229.

agwụ, in the sense of performative act); *ịsa aja* (obtaining knowledge about sacrifice; to be ordained a priest). These ideas are more or less embodied in the versions of initiation rites practised in the sub-cultural areas.

Being the only remedy to malignant possession, initiation is viewed with all the seriousness it deserves. It is a process for altering fortunes in favour of the individual. It provides healing and reconciles, on the one hand, the individual and *agwụ* and on the other, the individual and his society from which he may have become estranged because of the anti-social manifestations of pre-initiation possession. The institutions, namely, the diagnostic and medical which emerge as effects of initiation, are very useful and necessary for human survival.

We shall now consider two versions of the rite of *dibịa* initiation from two sub-cultural areas of Igboland namely, the southern and northern parts. The approach allows for the appreciation of ritual variations and adaptations which have occurred over the time. It also enables us to see how the essential motifs and the principal themes of the rites have been more or less maintained in both traditions.

Dibịa Initiation In Southern Igbo Area[4]

The first of the two major phases in *dibịa* initiation is known as *ịgbazu agwụ* through which an *agwụ* shrine is fully composed with the required pegs of the ritual plants and with the proper ritual ceremony. The shrine is the sacred space where a devotee accomplishes ritual encounters with *agwụ*. It is not only the *dibịa* who needs a shrine. Lower grades of *agwụ* devotees also need it as basic condition for obtaining favours from the spirit. In addition to this, such devotees may also be required to as nble some icons of *agwụ* attributes into a sacred basket. In that case, the first stage of the rite is also described as *itinye*

---

4   This account is based on interviews given by many diviners, healers and traditional heads among whom are Chief Oparaku Anyanwu, Patrick Anyanwu, Uzosike Njoku, Nzeji Alaribe, Nwogu Madugba and Jona Olo. Southern Igbo includes the areas of Owerri, Mbaise and Ngwa.

agwụ na abọ (putting *agwụ* into the basket). This first stage provides a suitable shrine around which the rites of the second phase take place.

First Phase of Initiation (*Ịgbazu agwụ*)

Essentially, the rites at this stage are intended to bring to completion the miniature shrine which came to existence with the rite of giving consent or saying yes to *agwụ* (*ikwenkwe agwụ*). The physical dimensions of the shrine are expected to conform more or less to the local standard. First of all, the intended area of the shrine is cleared of weeds and ritually defined as sacred by being marked with *ọmụ* (fresh palm twigs). Sixteen new pegs of *ogirisi* (Newbouldia Laevis) are added to the existing ones.

They are placed close to each other in rows of fours. While these represent *agwụ* and its attributes, other pegs are used to represent other members of the local pantheon in the act known as *ịgbanye mmụọ dị iche iche*. Hence in the shrine there are symbols for *Ala agwụ* (the Earth goddess of *agwụ*), *Ọbasị agwụ* (the god of *agwụ*), *Amadịọha/Kamalụ agwụ* (the god of thunder of *agwụ*), etc. The idea is that *agwụ* has need of these other spirit forces just as human beings have.

Agwụ has very well known ambivalent and capricious nature and in the establishment of the shrine, effort is made to eliminate or to subdue these qualities. The human party desires nothing but a spirit force that is benign, benevolent, honest and reliable. He does so with a rite aimed at expunging from the shrine, the negative character of *agwụ*. This is like exorcising the shrine.

These negative qualities known as *akaịkpa agwụ* or *ụrụala agwụ* are represented with a small chicken. Before the ceremony starts it is tethered to a pole within the space of the shrine. At the appropriate moment during the rite, a maternal uncle takes it away after the officiating *dibịa* has cursed and denounced it as *onye ọjọọ*, (the evil one) and ordered it to vanish. It is taken far away so that it could no longer find its way back. With this rite a mode of peaceful and harmonious relationship is believed to have been established at the shrine where sacrifices are offered to *agwu.* Thereafter, the devotee expects to encounter at the shrine the *agwu* that is auspicious. However, other rituals with the same objective show that no absolute guarantees of *agwu* single-mindedness and commitment to propitiousness may.ever be given.

The rite of *igbazu agwu* has also a contractual aspect. With their gods, devotees relate on the basis of *do ut des.* It is all the more called for in the case of *agwu* who is naturally prone to ambivalence. The contract is made on the authority of *ofo.* The officiating *dibia* pronounces the rights and duties of *agwu* and those of the human party. For erecting the shrine, offering sacrifices and for the intention to undergo the initiation, the person expects from *agwu,* good health, prosperity and good fortune in his undertakings. A typical contractual formula states:

Agwu a gbazuele gi.
I riele ohuru gi.
Nwoke a na-atu anya na i ga akwado aka oru ya,
Nye ya ahu isi ike,
Nye ya umu, aku na uba.

I gakwa ericha ohuru gi chefuo ya -
Ofo gbuo kwa gi.
I gakwa agba ya mgba okpuru -
Ofo gbuo kwa gi.
I gakwa ahu ihe oma biatara ya nochie uzo,
Ofo gbuo kwa gi.

Agwu your shrine is now completed.
You have received all that is due to you.
This man expects support in his undertaking,
Give him good health.
Give him children, and wealth.

If after receiving your rights and you forget him -
May *ofo* kill you.
If you betray him -
May *ofo* kill you.

If you block any good coming to him,
May *ọfọ* kill you.

The officiating *dibịa* who states the articles of the contract holds the *ọfọ* object in the right hand and whenever its name is mentioned he strikes it on the ground. Thus, the agreement is made. It is believed that anyone, man or spirit who reneges on an agreement pronounced solemnly with *ọfọ* has chosen the course to self-destruction.

The rite of *Ịgbazu agwụ* embodies references to two important human activities which *agwụ* superintends, namely divination and herbal medicine. *Anya afa* (the diviner's eye) and *anya nsị* (the healer's eye) are medicinal substances which are administered to the eyes of the initiate in anticipation of the future realization of his calling. Children who are present at this ceremony can also receive doses of the medicine as a way of conserving latent seeds of vocation to the *dibịa* profession. For older people, it is treatment against problems of the eyes, such as poor vision and eye-irritation.

Sacrifices of male and female fowls, kola nuts and libations are made to *agwụ* and the new shrine is thus consecrated and dedicated. With this rite the first phase of initiation is completed. The second part could follow immediately or much later, sometimes after many years, depending on when resources are available to the person.

Second Phase of Initiation Rite

The transformative rites in initiation fall into the second phase. Highly eloquent and intensive symbols are present which point to the change the candidate undergoes and the powers of priest, diviner and physician which he receives. As the ceremony progresses, the personal, social and religious dimensions of initiation gradually unfold.

Invitations and Announcement (oku agwụ)

When the *agwụ* which possesses a person has been identified as coming from the enate lineage, the maternal family is not simply notified and invited, its consent is also sought. It is believed that unless the aspirant obtains the approval and the blessings of his maternal family, the ceremony could run into several hitches. Moreover, as he presents gifts of palm wine, kola nuts, yams and fowls to his maternal family on this occasion, he receives, in return, the symbol object in confirmation of his maternal *agwụ* lineage.

The maternal family is pleased that its *agwụ* is being propagated through one of its own and when there are no serious reasons to do otherwise the family readily gives its approval. On the days of the initiation, the members take active part, not only by bringing gifts of food and drinks but also by supplying other forms of assistance to make sure the ceremony comes to a successful end.

Every initiate chooses a well experienced *dibịa* as sponsor, preferably any among his kin. It is usually the father or uncle if these are *dibịa*. Otherwise, any other *dibịa* from the community is chosen. The sponsor provides guidance and advice, and acts as an attendant in the course of the ceremony. It is his work to carry invitations to *mitini ụmụ dibịa* (the league of the *dibịa*) of the town and to introduce his candidate. He supervises the negotiations for fees to be paid, as well as directs his candidate through the session of scrutiny to determine if there are any impediments.[5] The *dibịa* league questions the candidate on his readiness to abide by the *dibịa* ethics. Thieves and persons convicted of breaking major taboos usually have to demonstrate

---

5   In the past, a stipulated amount of *ohu ikpeghe ano* (about 400 cowries) was paid as *ihu ego* (formal charge) in Nguru Mbaise. Each town association of the *dibịa* determined the fee paid for initiation. The money was usually shared out to all the *dibịa* in attendance at the initiation. Other requirements for the ceremony include 60 fowls, a ram, a male goat, three dogs, and many yams. Each *dibịa* usually received a life chicken to take home at the end of the ceremony.

real change of character before they could be considered eligible
for initiation. The support of relatives is important at initiation. The
candidate duly informs them by presenting gifts of palm wine
and kola nuts in the expectation that they would reciprocate by
giving him needed assistance. The women on their part organize
the provision of firewood and water and assist in preparing the
food for the feast. The men bring gifts of palm wine, yams and
kola nuts.

Seclusion Rite (*Iba ulo Agwu*)

The actual initiation begins with a seclusion rite (*iba ulo agwu*
and in the case of women initiation called *iru mgbede*), through
which a candidate undergoing initiation is set apart, hidden from
people, and as it were, turned invisible. This is achieved, first of
all, through disguises. He surrenders his normal clothing for a
piece of loin cloth. The hair of his head are completely shaven,
and his body coated with paste made from white chalk and red
earth. Fresh palm twigs (*omu*) are tied round his neck, wrists
and ankles. Then he is led into a place of seclusion known as *ulo
agwu* (*agwu* house) or *ulo afa* (divination house). [6]

The initiation usually begins on *Eke* and lasts for eight
days.[7] During this period, except for the need to fulfill other
ritual exercises when he could come outside, the candidate

---

6   The function of *omu* in this context is to designate the candidate as tabooed.
In the socio-religious and cultural application of *omu*, the intention is to
declare a person, thing or space, a prohibition. Any object on which *omu* is
placed is tabooed and may never be tampered with except with permission of
whoever placed it. There are several and even deeper symbolisms of *omu*.
"Young leaves or branches (*omu*) used to signify death, war; during some
ceremonies priests or those who are not expected to talk hold this between
their lips." (Cf. B. N. Okigbo, 1980 Ahiajoku Lecture, Culture Division,
Ministry of Information, Culture, Youth and Sports, Owerri, p.32).

7   With the eight-day Igbo week (the great, *Eke, Orie, Afo, Nkwo* and the small
Eke, Orie, Afo, Nkwo) the ceremony begins on the great *Eke* to end eight
days later on the next great *Eke*. Where the initiation ceremony lasts for four
days, it means that it begins either on the great *Eke* to end on the small *Eke*
or begins on the small *Eke* to end on the great *Eke*.

remains alone in the place of seclusion. Only the *dibia* who are protected by their own initiation could have contact with him. His wife and other members of the household are forbidden entrance into the place. The sponsor stays close enough to attend to him as the need arises. A female attendant is selected in the case of a woman's initiation.

The other regulations pertaining to the seclusion are equally stringent. The candidate must not sit on a chair or sleep on a bed. He sits and sleeps on the bare floor. He is forbidden to take a bath for the entire duration of the initiation. He may clean his hands with certain leaves after meals. The aim of such observances as Gennep has said is to separate the novice from his previous environment and to bring him into an incorporation with a new one.[8]

Rite to open the Eyes (Iwa Nkịta Anya)

At different times during the period of initiation, usually in the mornings and evenings, the initiate is subjected to the rite of *itu ọgwụ*, by which his eyes are doctored with medicine *(ọgwụ)*. The exercises are aimed at 'washing' and 'opening' the eyes of the candidate. He would normally be made to prostrate beside the shrine while the presiding *dibịa* pours spicy preparations into his eyes. No matter how terribly painful the treatment might be, he is expected to demonstrate manly stoicism.

One of the many sessions of this rite is called *iwa nkịta anya* (breaking the eye pupil). This takes place in *ọhịa mkpa* (the bad bush). The initiate is ceremoniously led into this place, usually at dawn, by a procession of the *dibịa*. A dog is taken along for sacrifice. The progress of the procession is announced by a rhythmic sound made by striking the shell of the tortoise and serves to warn any passers-by to keep a safe distance. The initiate holds a basket with which to carry herbs, roots, leaves and seeds collected in the bush and to be used in preparing medicine.

---

8   Van A. Gennep, *The Rites of Passage*, Routledge and Kegan Paul, London, 1977, p.81. First published in 1960.

At the middle of the forest, the initiate is made to lie on the back with his eyes held wide open. Then the dog is slaughtered and its blood as well as spicy concoctions are used to 'wash' his eyes. After the initial pains, the treatment is expected to act as sedative. As that happens all the presiding *dibịa* return home leaving the initiate all alone to find his way back on awaking.

The bad bush is a fear-inspiring place because evil spirits inhabit it. The dead who are denied burial and funerary rites because they have died of certain diseases are thrown into this place. The tabooed state of the initiate is all the more highlighted with this practice. He symbolically dies and is abandoned. In that period of 'death' and companionship with the dead and the evil spirits he masters the genius of their own world.

Sun Rite (Ịgba Ọbọ Anyanwụ)

The initiate, a presiding *dibịa* and a couple of assistants climb up the roof of the house at about midday when the sun is at its brightest. The purpose is to get closer to the sun and be exposed to the rays unobstructed by any object. The initiate lies on his back on top of the roof with the assistants helping to keep him in place. A cock is presented to the sun before it is slaughtered.

The blood is made to drip into the eyes and mouth of the candidate and into incisions made with a knife on his chest and thighs. Medicines are as well applied to his eyes until he becomes unconscious. He is then gently pushed off the roof to fall into the waiting hands of the *dibịa* on the ground. Still in an unconscious state, he is taken into the room and while he is being resuscitated with powerful stimulants all the people who are present, sing:

Nwa m gara ije,	My child who travelled,
Lọwa lọwa	Return home
Ibe gi alọla,	Your companions have come back,
Lọwa lọwa.	Return home.

Until the candidate is revived deep anxiety reigns. This is because some mischievous *dibịa* could direct dangerous spells on the candidate to make his revival very difficult or even impossible. None of the *dibịa* interviewed recalled an instance where there had been failure in resuscitating the initiate, yet they all spoke with apparent familiarity of some real cases.[9] The ritual replays the themes of death and rebirth. There is, however, no clear explanation of the symbolism of the sun. It is possible that here we have a remnant of some ancient rite of the sun that found its way into *dibịa* initiation.

Ritual Immunization (Ịgbusi Ahụ)

This rite requires the subjection of the person to a painful corporeal ordeal. From a boiling liquid of medicinal plants and other substances the candidate's body is sprinkled. While he feels severe pains, no burns or swellings are expected to appear. A sharpened machet is also dipped into the boiling medicine and while still hot it is used to make narrow incisions on parts of his body. But because the cuts are at once treated with special medicine, they heal immediately.

Thereafter, the *dibịa* is physically and spiritually fortified. It is said that he has been 'cooked on fire', 'fully baked' and 'hard boiled'. He is able to rebuff attacks of evil spirits and spirit forces, and to neutralize inimical magical spells of witches and sorcerers. The *dibịa* must be so furnished to be able to safely and effectively liberate other people when they become victims of such attacks.

Unearthing Ebi (ịbọ ebi)

After the preceding rites, a candidate is believed to have been effectively introduced into the realm of the supernatural such that he could exercise special powers. He is said to have acquired the 'third eye' and the power of extra sensory perception. He then could penetrate mysteries to untangle them, and could perceive events that occur in distant places. The rite to unearth the *ebi* gives the candidate the chance to exercise his new powers and

---

9 Female initiates are administered a modified form of this rite. It takes place not on the roof but in the space of the family reception room. This is because women according to custom are forbidden to get up to such heights.

before the people to earn the reputation of a transformed and spiritually empowered person.

Ebi is the symbol object of mystery and supernatural powers which is buried and hidden, somewhere, anywhere, far or near, and which the initiate sets out to discover and expose. But he must do this through meticulously retracing all the steps applied in hiding it. Usually it involves some complicated 'journey'. In the first place the *dibịa* who goes to bury the *ebi* makes several moves in many twisted directions.

He traces a route of several curves, climbs up trees, springs down, runs, crawls, walks on his hands and knees, frog-jumps, etc. The initiate receives great ovation if he is able to imitate each and every step to the point where the *ebi* is buried. He is then carried shoulder high. It is clear to all that the initiation has endowed the candidate with supernatuaral powers.

Packing the Sacred Basket (Ịkwa Abọ Agwụ)

At a stage during initiation, under the supervision of the presiding *dibịa*, the initiate assembles into a basket (*abọ agwụ*) the main symbols of *agwụ*. These include the statuettes of members of *agwụ* family namely, the male/husband, the female/wife, *agwụ* of maternal family, the son and the daughter. For any *dibịa*, the basket is precious and treated with much reverence because it is sacred. It contains the sacred images of *agwụ* itself. It will remain central in the *dibịa's* ritual and professional performances. In *ụlọ agwụ (agwụ* house) where the *dibịa* carries out his professional activities, the sacred basket takes a central place and is treated with great reverence.

When the *dibịa* has no *ụlọ agwụ*, he usually provides a place for the sacred basket in his bedroom. An informant narrated the story of a *dibịa* who had kept his basket carelessly and it was eaten up by termites along with all the sacred symbols it contained. *Agwụ* is said to have become so infuriated that the culprit was made to spend the rest of his life offering sacrifices of atonement. And yet *agwụ* brought him to a disgraceful end by letting him die in the market while it was in session.

Market Rites(ịpụ ahịa)

As the initiation approaches to an end, the initiate leaves the seclusion of *agwụ* house to present himself to the public in the market and to perform the market rites. These rites take place when the market is in full session and they serve two main purposes. First, they are acts of homage to the guardian spirits of the market place. Second, through the rites the entire community comes to know about the birth of a new *dibịa*.

The initiate carrying his ritual basket *(abọ agwụ)* is escorted to the market by the *dibịa* league, friends and relatives. The popular *ekpete* music of the *agwụ* cult is played for the procession. Palm wine and oil bean salad are taken along to the market for light refreshment.

The initiate and his companions go from one market corner to the other and at each of them he prostrates and receives spicy powdered medicine into his eyes. The powder is carried in a gourd *(nkụkụ ọgwụ)*. The candidate enjoys some liberties during the market rites. He picks any goods displayed for sale which please him and the owners must not complain nor try to stop him. They even count it as blessing for it is believed to bring good luck.

The mood of most *dibịa* who are present is not in the least sober. It is tuned up to reflect the rascality that is characteristic of *agwụ*. After the tour through the market, the candidate finally settles at the corner of the market shared by his village. Here he must prove to the public that he now has divinatory powers. This is called *ịgba afa ahịa* (market divination). There and then he is expected to display his ability to interpret *afa*. The crowd usually watches anxiously and raises ovation when the feat is successfully accomplished. The candidate is also tested on other matters to ascertain his possession of extra-sensory and prophetic powers.

Rite of Commitment to Dibịa-work Ethics (Ilo Obi Evule)

This rite is preceded by *ụra mmụọ* by which members of the *dibịa* group accompany the initiate to observe an entire night's vigil. The observance of a vigil points to the importance of this rite whose principal function is to get the new *dibịa* committed to the ethics that guide the practice of the vocation. Those who will not abide by the moral norms, such as the sorcerers and other evil-minded people, are not allowed to perform this rite. If any pretended otherwise and tried to do so it had always ended in failure. Unsuccessful candidates are taken to be evil people who have in mind the intention to apply their powers contrary to the ethical demands of saving life as laid down by the *dibịa* league. On account of the discredit that follows failure in this ordeal, only those who were sure of the purity of their intentions submitted to the rite.

The initiate spends the greater part of this night of vigil in prayers and reflections. His companions remain awake, warding off sleep with drinking and narrations of their many and varied experiences. The discussions centre on the significance of the imminent rite and the idea perhaps is to make the initiate appreciate the right weight of the matter. With the break of dawn, and before the immediate preparations are started for this rite, the candidate is formally examined and implications of *ilo obi evule* further explained to him.

Obi evule is prepared with the ram's heart. The ram is slaughtered for this specific purpose. The heart is taken and treated with medicine to prepare it for ingestion. Following local practices, other substances may also be added to it. In Ngwa area, *obi evule* is treated with the mnemonic substance known as *echewe echeta* (activator of the memory). It helps the recipient in the work of divination. In Mbieri, tiny metal pellets are mixed with the ram's heart. In doing this the ideas of strength particularly in moral matters are emphasized. In some other communities too, the hearts of other animals such as the he-goat or the dog could be added. The recipient of these parts is expected to reflect in his life as *dibịa* such positive attributes for which the animals have been valorized in religious rituals.

The candidate is expected to swallow the *obi evule*. He is not to bite it nor chew it. This object remains ever so intact in the recipient after it has been ingested. It is not digestible and it remains inside the *dibịa* for the rest of his life - an added organ so to say. The belief is that it is excreted only when the *dibia*'s time has come and he must die. So long as the *dibia* has this inside him, he enjoys immortality.

The high morality and strength of character expected of the *dibia* perhaps suggested the use of the ram which is highly evaluated as a metaphor for stoicism and strength. The *dibia* requires strength of character to remain faithful to the practice of 'good medicine' as against sorcerers. Then the linkage of *obi evule* to the life of the *dibia* makes the former a highly dynamic symbolism of *agwu* force.

Ablution

The end of the initiation is marked with an ablution. The candidate washes away the disguises and all the filth he has acquired in the duration of the initiation. When there is a stream or river nearby, this exercise takes place there. In that case sacrifices of a fowl, kola nuts and coins are made to the spirits of the river, so that they never would impede his work. After dressing in new clothes, the new *dibia* then presents himself to his community. He sits in front of his house to receive felicitations from relatives and friends. Many of them could only imagine what ordeal he had gone through to be made new and different from what he was. They all join to rejoice over his survival and success. It is said that he has stepped his feet on the land of the spirits.

Dibia Initiation In Northern Igbo Area[10]

Initiation in Northern Igboland is not a different system from that of the South. But the differences that separate the rites are important religious and cultural facts. What is equally interesting is that the versions have maintained enough features that establish them within the broader margins of Igbo religious culture.

---

[10] What is presented here is the model of initiation as found in Ihube, Okigwe, a town in northern Igbo area. The main sources are Uwakwe Onyeakobusi and Aforibe Nwankwo.

Invitation and Notices

The maternal family is the first to be considered with regard to invitations and notices in preparation for *dibịa* initiation . A keg of palm wine, kola nuts and a fowl are the gifts custom requires an aspirant to present for that purpose. The consent and blessings of the maternal family are considered indispensable for the initiation. In most cases of *agwụ* possession, *agwụ* of maternal family is reckoned to be primarily or secondarily involved. Any aspirant is therefore, expected to make this visit for the success of his initiation. The *dibịa* guild of the town are appropriately informed and consulted. This group approves the list of items to be provided for the rite. The aspirant under the direction of a kinsman who is a *dibịa*, presents the customary drinks and kola nuts to the guild during their meeting session. It is the guild that explains all that has to be done for a successful and valid initiation.

The aspirant must not fail to inform and invite his relatives as well as his friends. The relatives are expected to give material support to their kinsman to enable him properly entertain all the visitors. His shame, they know, is at the same time theirs.

Assembling Agwụ Symbols

Before the initiation begins the aspirant is required to acquire some important *agwụ* symbols. He obtains *ụkwụ agwụ*, (*agwụ* legs). *Ụkwụ agwụ* simply means the legs with which *agwụ* stands, walks and swiftly reaches its target. Its importance lies in the fact that it makes the vital affirmation of the existence of *agwụ*. It asserts that *agwụ* is not an imaginary reality. It is a true living being as its possession of legs could testify.

This symbol is fashioned with a pack of sticks taken from the roots of *ụdara* (Star apple/Chrysophylum Albidum). The roots are cut to equal sizes and encased with feathers. *Ụdara* is a tree that grows to a great height and size and provides one of the most popular fruits of Igboland. It is believed that it is particularly benign and in whatever cause it is employed, whether its roots, barks, leaves or fruits, it brings success. *Ụdara* is also a fertility plant and is, therefore, called *ụdara ọmụmụ.* The quest for an *agwụ* that is auspicious informed the preference of *ụdara* in this case.

The aspirant must also obtain wooden statuettes of members of *agwụ* household, namely, the male, the female consort, the offsprings that are male and female and the *agwụ* of the maternal family. A replication of the images with red clay is also required. At the end of the initiation, the clay images are permanently placed beside the shrine of *agwụ* under a shed of raffia mat. In recent times one observes that corrugated iron sheets which have become fashionable in building are used to replace the mats. The symbols carved on wood are usually kept in *agwụ* house or in the *dibịa's* own house if he does not yet own one.

Sacrifices

The aspirant provides the following to be used for various sacrificial rites: a dog, seven fowls, several kegs of palm wine, kola nuts and yams. After these animals have been slaughtered at the various instances, the flesh is used to prepare food for the feast. Each of the seven fowls is intended for a separate sacrifice. One is called *ọkụkọ isi anya* because it is killed right at the beginning of the initiation. It is presented with four yams. The second fowl that must be a cock is called *isugbe*. It is also presented with four yams and used for sacrifice during the erection of the shrine.

The third fowl is sacrificed to the ancestors. It must be a cock but one that has not started to crow, which is described as *otiri na nku ebeghi n'ọnụ.* The fourth fowl, also a cock is used in the preparation and empowerment of *ọgwụ* (medicine). This is also offered with four yams. The high point of the rite, that is, *ịtụ ọgwụ* (opening the eyes) requires a cock, a hen and the dog which are presented with eight yams. The last of the fowls is a little chicken which is offered to *Kamalụ,* the god of thunder. No clear explanation is given for this last sacrifice or why *Kamalụ* is involved in the matter. These are the minimal a candidate provides before the rite takes off. An affluent candidate may provide these in greater numbers and may even add other animals, which are not officially prescribed, in order to make the ceremony more remarkable.

The Shrine

Many of the activities of initiation are carried out around the shrine of *agwu* and so erecting and preparing one is a major undertaking preceding other rites of the initiation. When there is a miniature shrine existing from an earlier control ritual measure, it suffices to enlarge it with new pegs of ritual plants, particularly *ogirisi, abosi* and *oha*. The officiating *dibia* directs the placing of the various pegs. Each group of pegs has a name and specific symbolic importance. A group of pegs of *abosi* may represent *ukwu agwu* (*agwu* legs) while another group of *ogirisi* stands for *ndi azu agwu* (*agwu* ancestors). One or a group of *ogirisi* pegs may designate *akanri agwu* (the right hand of *agwu*, positive influences) and another set of *oha* pegs may represent *akaikpa agwu* (left hand of *agwu*, negative influences).

Echuchuu and *ebubeagu* are ritual plants that are commonly used for enriching and furnishing shrines. It is believed that through the erection of the shrine and the planting of the ritual plants, *agwu* is rendered much more controllable especially with regard to the negative effects. A few stone blocks are arranged behind the pegs on top of which are placed the clay images of *agwu*. The shrine is dedicated with the sacrifice of a fowl *(isugbe)*, yams, dry fish, white and yellow chalk.

Venerating Ancestors

Trays woven with palm fronds known as *igboaja* are used to present to the ancestors of each village of the town, portions of the sacrifice of fowls. On the road to each village, a tray is placed. The purpose is to notify the ancestors of the initiation in order to obtain their authorization and goodwill. They are called upon to watch over the initiation ceremony and ward off any disasters. The idea also is to reverence the ancestors who originated the religious practices and left them for their progenies.

Preparation of Medicine

Fruits of such plants as *ụda, ụzịza* and *ose* which are spicy; various other leaves and roots with similar quality, make up the assemblage of medicinal materials which are used in preparing the spicy substances for washing and opening the eyes of the initiate. The medicines used for such transformative rituals as in initiation, until they are ritually empowered have no effectiveness. The process of ritual empowerment known as *ịwake ọgwụ* consists, in this case, in sacrificing a fowl at the shrine of *agwụ* and sprinkling the medicine with the blood. Some alligator pepper are chewed and spat on the medicine while the officiating *dibịa* states solemnly the effects desired from the medicine.

Symbolization of Death

The beginning of initiation is ritually announced with the action known as *ịtụ anwụ*. The presiding *dibịa* makes this announcement by taking up a gourd stuffed with feathers, pieces of kola nuts and alligator pepper, and breaking it by throwing it on the ground in front of the aspirant's house. The contents scatter in different directions. The image of destruction and death is clearly evident. Initiation is after all a destruction of the old self. The words he says after this suggest also the idea of a rebirth midwifed by *agwụ*:

*Agwụ amụgbule onye ukwu
Amụgbule onye nta.*

Agwụ mid-wife safely the great person
Mid-wife safely the small person.

Prayers which embody contrasts, such as the great and the small recall the all inclusive cosmic reality. The prayer is therefore, a wish for universal good and in this case the mind dwells longer on the candidate who is being initiated.

Initiation Proper (*Igwo Agwu*)

The preceding steps are only preparations leading to the main rites of *dibia* initiation. The aims of initiation are to free the individual from malignant effects of *agwu*, to transform him, and confer on him the spiritual powers that he needs to function as *dibia*. It normally begins on the evening of *Eke* market day and ends on *Orie*, the following day.

The candidate dresses in loin cloths. His hair is completely shaven and his body disguised with coatings of pastes of white chalk, yellow chalk and red clay. He is brought to lie supine at the shrine with the wooden and clay statues of *agwu* lined up on his head side. Assistants who are *dibia* hold him in position while spicy medicine is poured into his eyes. He must not show feelings of pain. The dog and the fowl are slaughtered and the blood spilled over him and into his eyes, mouth and ears. The officiating *dibia* articulates the intentions of the rite in a prayer addressed to *agwu*. As he does this he holds the *ofo* with the right hand.

Agwu, nwa gi a emejuputala ihe a na atu anya n'aka ya.
O nyele gi nkita, nye gi okuko.
O nyele gi oji, nye gi mmanya.
O tuola gi, O kpobatala gi ulo
Ugbu a o rule gi n'aka:

Nye ya umu; nye ya oganihu.
Buru ya agwu udo, agwu aku n'uba
Ikpo ya igwo ogwu, gosi ya ezi mgborogwu
Ma ehihie ma uchichi
Ikpo ya igba afa, too nti n'ala ma o kpo gi
Gi na ya, onye ga-igho ibe ya aghugho
Ofo gbuo kwa ya - ihaa
Ofo gbuo kwa ya - ihaa
Ofo gbuo kwa ya - ihaa

(*Agwu*, this child of yours has fulfilled all expected of him. He has given you the dog, given you the fowl.

He has given you kola, given you wine.
He has made images of you, and made a home with you
Now it is your turn:

Give him children; give him progress.
Be to him the *agwu* of peace, the *agwu* of wealth.
If you call him to be healer,-
show him the right herbal roots.
Both in the day and in the night.
If you call him to be diviner,-
listen to him when he invokes you.
You and he, whoever deceives or cheats the other-
May the *ofo* kill him - *ihaa*
May the *ofo* kill him - *ihaa*
May the *ofo* kill him - *ihaa)*

The prayer ends with the enunciation of the conditions of coexistence between *agwu* and the *dibia*.[11] At every mention of the word *ihaa* (may it be so), the officiating *dibia* taps the *ofo* gently on the ground. A pact is thus made.

---

[11] It is very well known that the idea of reciprocity permeates traditional religiosity. Commenting on the Igbo attitude towards the gods, Echeruo said: "We respect the gods, but as the proverb says, we also expect the gods to respect us humans. We acknowledge the power of the gods, and cultivate that power, but when these gods consistently fail to prove themselves powerful we reserve the right to discard them and seek out new gods." (Cf. Michael J. C. Echeruo, 1979 Ahiajoku Lecture, p.18). Responding to the comments that the Igbo do not care for their gods, Nwoga said: "...the Igbo should be recognized as caring very much for their gods - but only as long as those gods are effective. Any god that becomes useless has no right to pect the Igbo to continue to serve him since the essence of godhead is ,ower". (Cf. Donatus Ibe Nwoga, 1984 Ahiajoku Lecture, p.19). Beattie has observed that this attitude is widespread in African societies: "Where the relationship between men and spirits is conceived in this way, as it is in many parts of Africa, its reciprocity is made quite explicit in the invocations used. If prayer is associated with sacrifice, as it usually is, the spirit's attention is drawn to the beast or other object which is being sacrificed to it; a hint that it should accept its reciprocal obligation to do what it is asked." (Cf. John Beattie, *Other Cultures*, p.233).

Seclusion

The initiate is then led into the seclusion of *ụlọ agwụ* (*agwụ* house). Now the earlier disguise of his physical state is rendered much more poignant by the reddish blood of ritual victims which has been poured on him. In a more intensive manner he represents danger. All through the night he is to remain in this place separated from the rest of the society. He sleeps on the bare floor and is forbidden any kind of ablution or contact with women. In the morning he takes a bath, dresses up for the warm embraces of older colleagues, friends and relatives. The rest of the day is given to feasting.

Certification of Vocation

The new *dibịa* confirms his calling as diviner by throwing the *afa* and observing the fall. This is repeated for four consecutive days. If the *afa* beads fall on the concave side at most of the trials the vocation is confirmed, otherwise he may never take up divination.

Interpretation Of Some Themes In *Dibịa* Initiation

The various models of *dibịa* initiation found in Igbo sub-cultural areas have many things in common. It can be said that each and every one of them embodies similar symbols and this may explain why a *dibịa* from one part is recognized in any other part of Igboland. There are common themes, and paradigms. The purpose of any given ritual is accomplished through the application of symbols namely, actions, words, gestures, and objects. These symbols uphold the various themes which are intended by the participants to be made explicit. That they are able to perform these functions is the result of the conventional values which they are assigned.

The *dibịa* initiation rite has some similarities with other rites of passage such as the rite of initiation into adulthood, especially in their thematic expressiveness. Each rite must order its symbols so as to bring the best effective articulation to the themes of the initiation. We shall see this being realized as we consider some themes of *dibịa* initiation.

The Mythical Theme

The celebration of the myth which undergirds the dogma and rituals of the *agwụ* cult occurs at different instances. The double-origin theory of *agwụ*, by which in most cases of *agwụ* possession, the agnate and enate agents are present ordains that initiation be preceded by visits to one's maternal family. Gifts of fowls, wine and kola nuts are presented at the visit. On its part the maternal family gives the aspirant cult relics, such as a statuette of *agwụ* or *nkuku ọgwụ*. The agnate family is also outstandingly informed. This is all the more necessary if the tradition exists that children inherit their parents' *agwụ* symbols.

At another instance, the ambivalent character of *agwụ* which is explained as a union of *agwụ ọma* (positive) and *agwụ ọjọọ* (negative) explains such rituals of expunction intended to bring about integrity in *agwụ* personality. The expectation from a post-initiation period is the *agwụ* of wholesomeness, devoid of malignancy and ambiguity. The use of a chicken to represent the negative *agwụ* is a common practice. Although fowls are not negatively or lowly valorized in rituals, the use of the little chicken is intended to express sentiments of contempt, disdain and rejection for the negative character of *agwụ*.

In another form, the rite for controlling *agwụ* ambivalence and capriciousness consists in inserting certain ritual pegs at the shrine during the rite of erecting the *agwụ* shrine. These pegs known as *ụrụ agwụ/agwụ arụkwala mụ ụrụ (agwụ* don't trick me) are intended to be constant reminders to *agwụ*, of the ethics of this new relationship. Another force which is introduced in the rite as check to capriciousness and deceit is the *ọfọ*. Most *dibịa* do agree that the effect of the rites of expurgation is highly limited, for in actual fact, post-initiation period is never completely rid of *agwụ* intrigue and ambivalence. What the rite definitely assures is some manageable situation.

The Sacred

Initiation is essentially a religious activity and various elements of the rite are eloquent on that. Time, space, actions and persons which are characterized with degrees of sacredness converge to make the entire initiation an intensively sacred exercise.

Time

Eke market day is most generally observed as sacred to *agwụ*. In some areas some specialists also observe *Nkwọ*. On such a day, the *dibịa* avoids consultations. It is believed that works of divination and healing turn out badly if undertaken on such a day. The *agwụ* minister therefore, attends to his other domestic and social matters. Initiation starts usually on the evening of *Eke* to end eight days later on the next *Eke* except where the rite lasts for just one day. Because initiation is a sacred undertaking it is fixed to commence on the day sacred to the deity.

Space

The focal point in the rite of initiation is the shrine. As our accounts very well have explained, care is taken to build it to satisfy a standard which is believed to have been so revealed by the spirit from time immemorial. The location and arrangement of the shrine has not been left entirely in the hands of humans to determine. A shrine is primarily the result of divine action. According to Beattie it is a divine command where and how it is, built;

> As a rule, spirits are conceived as immaterial and usually, as being diffused through space, or perhaps as not in space at all. But they are generally associated with specific places in the material world. If these places are made by men, usually at the behest of a god or spirit, they are called shrines.[12]

The shrine is sacred and is very well distinguished from normal space. Its sacredness is pointed out by the many taboos which are observed for it. Any one who has a shrine watches out for any defiling actions or objects in its vicinity. It is absolutely forbidden to urinate or defecate on a shrine. The priest pays close attention to the spiritual and physical regulations which he must observe especially before worship at the shrine.

---

12 John Beattie, *Other Cultures*, p.232.

There are many traditions regarding the arrangement of the ritual plants at the shrine. The ritual pegs may be placed in a circular or a semi-circircular form, or placed in parallel rows. The practice differs from place to place and from one *dibịa* to another. About the practice in Nimo Thomas recounted that;

> . . . eight *ogilisi* pegs are cut and one big piece, four smaller ones are tied at each end of the latter, another peg is put a little distance away as *Ikenga* . . ., another is *isi agu [agwụ]*, head of *agu [agwụ]*; the main piece is called *ekwensu agu [agwụ]*; a fowl is sacrificed to it, which children eat, together with all vegetables, which children however, do not eat.[13]

In Nri, the shrine is arranged in four parallel rows of *ogirisi* pegs which curve into a semicircle. Each unit of four pegs represents one of the four personality units of *agwụ* household: the male, the female, the offsprings and *agwụ* of the maternal home. In many parts of Southern Igboland, the circular arrangement prevails. In this case sixteen pegs are put around the earlier ones of the rite of *ekwele m agwụ*, that might have revived and become shrubs. Other rìtual plants other than *ogirisi* which are used include, *abọsị, ọha* and *echuchuu*.

It is also common practice to place a small clay bowel at the shrine. Certain offerings for the spirit such as kola nuts, alligator pepper or money may be dropped into this bowel. Generally, priests use objects or other plants at their shrines for reasons of enriching its image and aura. The shrine provides the suitable sacred space for the initiation. Here sacrifices are made to the spirit. Here too, the initiate prostrates for the transformative rituals which open his eyes to a new world of realities. Henceforth, he seeks the benevolence of this spirit in the mystery and sacredness of his shrine.

Sacrifice

Sacredness as the character of the initiation is highly accentuated by the sacrificial rites. There are sacrifices with a variety of

---

13 Northcote W. Thomas, *Law and Custom of the Iba of the Awka Neighbourhood S. Nigerid*. p. 39.

items: rams, goats, dogs, fowls, kola nuts, alligator pepper, white and yellow chalk. Libations of wine are poured profusely. Sacrifices are made at different locations such as the bad bush, the roof of the house and the cross roads. They all form a continuum that express the deep religious quality of initiation.

Sacred Persons

The *dibịa*- priests, diviners and religious healers - constitute the core of the assembly at the initiation. These are the religious specialists who by virtue of their initiation and work are protected by taboos which define their sacred statuses. Their presence contributes to the sacred character of initiation.

The Transcendental Theme

Reference to the transcendent is prominent with three groups of realities of initiation. These are the icons, *ọgwụ* (medicine) and the *dibịa*. The display of icons representative of the spirit creates a very intensive presence of it. In Uturu, a northern Igbo town, the production of the clay images of *agwụ* during the initiation is accompanied with prayerful address to the figures which seems to overlook their sheer symbolic status.

> *'Elegbuo, elegbuo',*
> *Ọ wụkwa ya anwụla anwụ*
> *Bụrụ ya agwụ udo*
> *Bụrụ ya agwụ ọmụmụ*
> *Apụla ya ụpụ awara*
> *Ọnọ na miri ahụ ụzọ*
> *Ururu mgbadu ụzọ . . .*

> As you cast your spell,
> let him not die
> Be for him the *agwụ* of peace
> Be for him the *agwụ* of fertility
> Do not make him wander aimlessly about
> You that see clearly in water
> You, *ururu* (rodent) of the path way. . .

There is another perspective to the transcending quality of the artistic symbols. This arises from the fact that they are not taken to be sheer arbitrary creations of the artist. Religious art is the result of both divine and human effort. It is the deity who reveals himself to the human mind. The transcendent quality of the rite of initiation is, therefore, given strong eloquence with the presence of the divine images.

Transcendental power is recalled and celebrated with *ọgwụ* (medicine) and its applications. The species of flora, fauna, insects and reptiles which have healing power are taken to have been so endowed by God for the benefit of man. Before its application, *ọgwụ* is formerly and ritually empowered through consecration, and charged with spiritual force.

The transformation of an initiate's faculties is accomplished through the application of *ọgwụ*. The eyes, for instance, are washed with *ọgwụ* to enable him to see spirits, perceive and penetrate hidden realities. *Ọgwụ* embodies forces which can destroy, heal, transform, rebuild or empower. The initiate experiences the diverse powers of *ọgwụ* in his initiation and finds them overpowering and surpassing.

The *dibịa* symbolizes, in a strong way, the transcendent force. He is compared to *mmọnwụ* (the masquerade) the spirit of the ancestor. Ordinary people who contest with him make fatal mistake. During the dramatic display of *ọgwụ* at some stage of initiation at Uturu, accompanying songs acknowledge and praise the supernatural qualities of the *dibịa*. They declare that only the masquerade can safely shake hands with the *dibịa*[14]

Chorus: *A na-ekwe mọnwụ n'aka?*
Ikwe mọnwụ n'aka
Ikwere ọnwụ n'aka eh
A na-ekwe mọnwụ n'aka?

---

[14] Song recorded during an interview given by Mishark Uhuohuo at Achara Uturu.

Nkuku eze dibịa adawala ịjaghịrịja - Chorus
Nkwe dibịa n'aka, ekwe mmọnwụ n'aka eh -
Nna Okeọma ekwe dibịa n'aka eh -
Jadum Jadum ọfọ dị ire -
Nkuku eze dibịa bịa gwọọ nke m hụrụ n'anya -

Chorus: Does one shake hands with the masquerade?
Whoever shakes hand with the masquerade
Incurs death through hand-shaking
Does one shake hands with the masquerade?

The sound from the medicine gourd is *Ijaghịrịja* - Chorus
Shaking hands with the *dibịa* is shaking hands with the masquerade-
Our ancestor Okeoma shakes hand with the *dibịa*-.
Jadum Jadum ọfọ which is potent
The medicinal gourd of the chief *dibịa* cure that which I see-

The transcending power of the *dibịa* is given expression with *Ikiri,*, a symbol object of the ball of fire which is seen especially in the night flying across the sky. It is explained that when the *dibịa* has a long distance to travel and especially if he foresees danger on the road, he easily transforms himself into a comet. The *dibịa* is able to do this because of the supernatural powers which he possesses.

The Liminal State

The liminal state features in many rites of passage especially in the case of passage rite to adulthood. It is also quite prominent in the *dibịa* initiation. This state involves a period of separation and isolation for the initiate as he undergoes the trauma of symbolic death and rebirth. This exercise is so central to the entire rite whose major focus is the creation of a new reality with the passage of a man into the possessed state of the *dibịa*.

The initiate is introduced into the liminal or marginal state beginning with the transformation of his physical appearance through the application of disguises. This is achieved through such acts as shaving, shedding normal clothing, putting on the body pastes of white chalk and red mud, and painting the eyelids with yellow chalk. The ankles, wrists and neck are tied with fresh palm twigs. These applications set the initiate apart as a prohibition. The effect of the disguise corresponds to what Turner has described as;

> the first level of separation [which] comprises symbolic behaviour signifying the detachment of the individual or group either from an earlier fixed point in the social structure or a set of cultural conditions (a "state").[15]

The usual place of seclusion is the *agwụ* house. This is normally a hut built specifically in the homestead for the purpose. Where none exists, any chosen room in the house where the initiate lives, serves as an acceptable alternative. The danger which the initiate in this seclusion poses is indicated by the taboos which he observes and which others observe for him. Contact with non-initiates, especially sexual, are forbidden. The initiate eats food prepared by specially appointed people such as virgins or women who have passed child-bearing age and such sumptuous meals are cooked with distinctive ingredients. Only those who have been initiated can safely enter the *agwụ* house or communicate with the initiate. With the rest of the uninitiated, contact is dangerous. As Mary Douglas explains:

> danger lies in transitional states, simply because transition is neither one state nor the next, it is undefinable. The person who must pass from one to another is himself in danger and emanates danger to others. The danger is controlled by ritual which precisely separates him from his old status, segregates him for a time and then publicly declares his entry to this new status...."[16]

---

15 Victor Turner, *Betwixt and Between: The Liminal Period in Rites de Pass* ', in William A. Lessa and Evon Z. Vogt, (eds.) *Readers in Compara Religion*, Harper & Row Publishers, New York, 1979, p.235. This p. appeared first in 1964, in the Proceedings of the American Ethnologic ai Society Symposium on New Approaches to the study of Religion.

16 Mary Douglas, *Purity and Danger: An Analysis of Concepts of Pollution and Taboo*, Routledge and Kegan Paul, London, 1966, p.96.

Ray, who has carried out a study of rituals in Africa has also described this state as a very critical one. He explains that those in such state,

> are neither what they were nor what they will become. Initiates are neither children, nor adults, male nor female, human nor animal. They are momentary anomalies, stripped of their former mode of being, ready to become something new.[17]

Turner describes such state as structural invisibility by which the initiate is "no longer classified and not yet classified."[18] The liminal state of the initiate, Turner also explains, is represented by symbols drawn from biology of death, decomposition, catabolism and other physical processes that have a negative tinge.[19]

These are prominent themes in *dibia* initiation. The theme of death is symbolized with such practices that condemn the initiate to sitting and sleeping only on the floor during the liminal period, for he must indeed identify with the earth. Filthy practices that forbid him to bath or to wash his hands after using them at meals, even when the rite would last as long as eight days, typify the symbolic act of dying and putrefaction.

The process of symbolic death in *dibia* initiation terminates in the event of symbolic birth. The ablution marks the end of seclusion and the emergence of the *dibia*. The 'old man' gives place to the 'new man' and not without certain death. Very aptly therefore, Turner describes the house of seclusion as representing both the tomb and the womb.[20]

The Transformation Theme

There are those ritual episodes as *igbusi ahụ*, and *itụ anya*, whose purposes are transformative. They are physical actions tied to spiritual ends. They are 'sacraments'. In most cases

17 B. C. Ray, *African Religions: Symbol, Ritual and Community*, Prentice-Hall, New Jersey, 1976, p.91.
18 Victor W. Turner, *"Betwixt and Between: The Liminal Period in Rites de Passage"*, p.236.
19 *Ibid.*
20 *Ibid.*, p.237.

severe bodily pain is involved and it is expected to bring about
spiritual result.

Ịgbusi ahụ means hardening the body or fortifying it and
ultimately making the *dibịa* invulnerable to all sorts of external
inimical attacks that could be magical, spiritual or sorcerous. It
protects the *dibịa* also from dangers that arise from contact with
persons in the liminal state.

Ịtụ anya (to open the eyes) which is an outstanding
transformative rite occurs several times during the initiation and
at different locations such as the shrine, the bad bush, the roof
top or the market place. The purpose at each instance is the
same, although in an ever increasing intensity expected to reach
perfect fulfillment at the instance of *ịwa nkịta anya* (breaking the
eye pupil). The rite of opening the eyes sums up the whole
exercise of initiation. It enables the *dibịa* to possess the prophetic
spirit and to foresee the future, to see the messages embodied in
the fall of the *afa* and to interpret them.

The *dibịa* sees those herbs which spirits reveal in dreams
and trances. He is able to discover hidden realities, to see and
meet spirits with no adverse consequences to his person. In
other words, it opens up the senses to make them capable of
perceiving and experiencing reality at a level hidden from
ordinary people. Physical encounter with spirits is taken as
regular experience of the *dibịa* after the eyes have been opened.
"Once in a while, the spirits of ancestors came down as guests to
the human world. Diviners saw them and mortals in lonely
afternoons or darkness of the night saw them, or even bumped
into spirits with dire consequences."[21] In Mbieri, the values of
ịtụ anya are put into a song used during initiation or other feasts
of *agwụ*.[22]

---

[21] Ogbu C. Kalu, Religion and Social Control in Igboland, in Jacob K.
Olupona and Sulayman S. Nyang (eds.), *Religious Plurality in Africa: Essays
in Honour of John S. Mbiti*, Mouton de Gruyer Berlin, 1993, p.115.

[22] Song recorded during interview granted by Nwatamole, a diviner, on
15/3/92.

Chorus: *Owe owe owe*
           Ewu nwe egbere owe

Aga m atụ ya anya	I will open your eyes - Chorus
Anya e ji eri ji	Eyes to eat yam with
Anya e ji akpa akụ	Eyes to make wealth with
Anya e ji ahụ ụzọ	Eyes to see with
Aga m atụ ya anya	I will open your eyes
Ụmụdibịa abịala	The *dibịa* have come
Ụmụdibịa abịalanụ	The *dibịa* have really come
Anyị tewe egwu	Let us dance
O rule mgbe ọ labụ	It is at such a time
Madụ ama ebe ya	One knows oneself
O rule mgbe ọ labụ	It is at such a time
Nwanyị amara di ya	The woman respects the husband
Enyimma	My good friend
Ụmụdibịa abịala	The *dibịa* have come.
Enyimma . . .	My good friend . . .

The inner and spiritual transformation which the *dibịa* undergoes opens up to him the way to the spiritual world of powers and endows him with tremendous potentials which are fully realized in the situation of sound training and harmonious relationship with his deity. His ability to read the medium correctly and his efficiency in the use of therapeutic substances may improve according to the state of his natural gifts, such as intellectual alertness. In the subsequent chapter we shall examine the complementary relationship between initiation and other aspects of human natural development.

Chapter 5

Significance and Consequences of *Dibịa* Initiation

New Personality and New Role

The purpose of initiation into the cult of *agwụ* is to end the first and negative phase of possession and to bring about a second and a positive one. The contrasting pictures of pre-initiation and post-initiation conditions spell this out clearly. The application of the term possession to both phases underscores the ambivalence characteristic of the possessing agent.

A person in the first phase of possession is called *onye agwụ na-akpa* or *onye agwụ na-enu*. These descriptions do not ordinarily suggest an indwelling of a spirit. Remedial rites are not of the nature of exorcism but of control measures. For that purpose, there are *ịrụ agwụ* (fastening *agwụ*) or *ike akọ na uche* (tying intelligence and wisdom). *Ịrụ agwụ* through which the spirit is localized and restricted provides the sacred environment within which it is reached and propitiated.

Through initiation, the *dibịa* becomes one who has knowledge of *agwụ* and *agwụ* matters (*ịsa agwụ*). He is also one who has knowledge of sacrifice (*ịsa aja*) and so one who is ordained. The *dibịa*'s eyes have been opened (*ịtụ anya*), and he has been cured of *agwụ* afflictions (*ịgwọ agwụ*). This new state is rightly described as possession because the healing episodes of the initiation, and its contractual and transformative rites generate the type of relationship between the man and the spirit, which is harmonious and positive, but one in which the human party is under the control of the spirit.

Rather than the idea of a mere indwelling of a spirit in the possessed, that of a relationship arising from some form of incorporation between them is more strongly expressed. The ritual object, *obi evule* which the *dibia* swallows during initiation remains in him, perfectly intact and undigested, throughout his life. It is incorporated in the human host to represent a vital spiritual power or faculty. This is a notion Amara explains:

> ... in magic and religion habitation does not seem to be enough. The spirit, though foreign originally, is incorporated into the body and they both become one. The relationship is more permanent and endows lasting powers of prophecy, divination or mastery in the art of altering natural phenomenon.[1]

It is believed that the characteristic ambivalence of *agwu* makes it possible to suppress originally malignant effects and substitute them with positive endowments. In pre-initiation possession, the situation of indwelling is not believed to obtain. Most *dibia* perceive this state as one in which a person is under the influence of the spirit that is nonetheless, external to him. On the contrary, post-initiation possession entertains the view of incorporation of the spiritual agent.

The *dibia* receives the positive divine influences as the improved performances of his senses and psychic faculties. Feats that had proved impossible now become possible. As the situation might demand, *agwu* dominates, impels, propels, guides and teaches the *dibia* and enhances his work. Nwoga has explained that;

> ... divination is not just physical or psychological manipulation of clients but a genuine process of gaining access to the abstract world of events of the past and the future and bringing back information on which one may act with confidence. The eyes that see into the past and future should also see into the present and that is why a genuine diviner is not supposed to ask the client what the problem is with which he has come.[2]

Most *dibia* we interviewed claimed experience of one or more powers of the extra-sensory perception, such as precognition, telepathy or clairvoyance. There are those who strongly assert their ability to detect corporal and spiritual problems of clients by simple visual contact. Others claim to be able to predict with accuracy, the number of persons that would come in a particular day to consult them, as well as the nature of their complaints. All these are possible because the eyes of the *dibia* are opened. Accounts of the feats the *dibia* are reputed to accomplish were so well known that Isichei concluded they could not all have been mere empty claims. "I think", she said;

> that it is possible that Igboland's *dibia* were developing real skill - or sciences - in the sphere of what we would now call extra-sensory perception.[3]

Some *dibia* experience changes of psychic and somatic types which are not naturally accounted for. The *dibia's* eyes could turn reddish, or he could become aware of the feeling of being overcome by some invisible force. Such experiences, an informant explained, usually herald divination to untie very intricate matters or a healing episode involving combat against some stubborn spirits or their agents.[4] Okoro Kalu, a renowned *dibia* claimed that some invisible and overwhelming force guide. him to places where agents of evil spirits and sorcerers have buried dangerous medicine.

The initiated is aware that he is in the possessed state. His eyes have been opened and he no longer finds mysteries to be mysterious. He knows he has the 'third eye' and sees what ordinary mortals are incapable of seeing. The scales that had blocked his sight have been removed and he begins to make visual penetrations into the realm of the supernatural world and into the hidden realities of other people's lives.

The *dibia* in his person and work makes vital contributions in his community. Crowther, one of the earliest missionaries of Igboland, had noted that "the priest in particular through whom

---

3 Elizabeth Isichei, *A History of the Igbo People*, Macmillan, London, 1976. p. 124.

4 Cf., Doctor John Chima Ama, Oral interview. Some other *dibia* questioned on these issues confirm they are common experiences of most *dibia*. In the case of exorcism, spirits that have been expunged might direct their anger on the exorcist and this is why a good *dibia* must be an *'okpoka'*, that is, one who is strongly fortified.

the gods speak as their oracles, whose word must not and cannot be denied are in fact the chief ruling power . . ."[5] The *dibịa* earn respect through the services they offer which their communities find very important. Elizabeth Isichei has mentioned some of the essential socio-religious functions of the *dibịa*:

> He explained the supernatural face of events, and he made misfortune intelligible, and so acceptable. He prescribed the sacrifices which would control the activity of supernatural beings. In some cases, disputing parties would have recourse to one of Igboland's regional network of oracles, such as the *Agbala* of Awka, or *Ibini Ukpabe*, at Arochukwu.[6]

The *dibịa* provides guidance to his community for as it is commonly believed "the diviner is the light of every community, and where there is none, the people grope through darkness to doom."[7] This is the logical conclusion based on the function of the diviner as the interpreter of events in individual and community lives. The Igbo aptly express this with the proverb: *a na-esi na anya dibịa ahụ ndị mmụọ* (one sees the spirits through the eyes of the *dibịa*). His crucial role in society in terms of leadership and stability hinge on the fact that people repose much trust in him and tend to follow his prescriptions and respect his predictions especially if he is well reputed. The *dibịa ọgwụ* (the healer) takes on the role of saviour especially in times of major communal crisis such as war or outbreak of epidemics. Besides administering medicines to the sick, he prepares the amulets *(ekike)* for protection of people and property, against evil spirits and evil people. In normal times, the work of the *dibịa* brings him, more than anyone else, in contact with other members of the society.[8]

---

5   Cf. Crowther's Report on the Niger Mission, 1875. In *Church Missionary Intelligence*, 1876, p. 472. In F.K. Ekechi, *Missionary Enterprise and Rivalry in Igboland* 1857 - 1914, Frank Cass, London, p.17.

6   Elizabeth Isichei, *A History of the Igbo People*, p. 24.

7   M. Y. Nabofa and Ben Elugbe, "Epha: Urhobo System of Divination and its Esoteric Language". *Orita: Ibadan Journal of Religious Studies*, XXX/1, June 1981, p.3.

8   John S. Mbiti describes the medicine-man as one who "acts not only as a doctor but often as a listener to people's troubles of all kinds and as their counsellor or adviser. When cattles die, their owners go to him for help;

While the *dibia* guild of a locality is not a political or judicial organization, it has bylaws to regulate the conduct of the members. Indirectly the guild promotes common good, peace and social order. The association contributes to the stability of the society also by minimizing competition and conflict through upholding the initiation rites as prime requirement for becoming a *dibia*.

Training

The diviner or physician must be versed in theoretical and practical knowledge about the profession. He is expected to have in-depth knowledge of the materials he uses in his work and of observances that regulate their applications. Such knowledge is not conferred by initiation. Often, the training is antecedent to initiation and what the latter could be said to do is to effect the ritual legitimization of the knowledge, a condition that

---

when children disobey parents, the parents go to him for advice; when someone is going on a journey, he consults the medicine-man to know whether or not the journey will be a success or to obtain protective medicines, and so on. . . . They pray for their communities, take the lead in public religious rituals, and in many ways symbolize the wholeness or health of their communities. . . ." (Cf. *Introduction to African Religion*, pp. 152-3). As Igbo culture came into contact with European culture and Christianity, the role of the *dibia* in society, from the ethical perspective of Christianity began to be viewed, as wicked and inimical to human welfare. The Christian missionaries saw the *dibia* as the agent of Satan. Referring to the human instruments to accomplish evil in the world, Jordan considered the *dibia* the worst of them all. He acknowledged however, that not all of them were evil. "But when a town was really debased, many of the *dibias* [*ndi dibia*] in it were certainly instigators of crime, because they were responsible for ordering and conducting the many kinds of sacrifice, including human sacrifice. If a calamity occurred, the *dibia* was consulted as to the proper action to be taken towards appeasing the spirits; if he declared that a human victim was needed then a human victim was procured, so the amount and type of the crimes in any town were largely traceable to the actions of *dibias* [*ndi dibia*], who certainly in this matter were the chosen instruments of Satan." (Cf. John P. Jordan, *Bishop Shanahan of Southern Nigeria*, Conmore & Reynolds, Dublin, 1948, pp. 154-5). Such powers show how important the *dibia* was to his community. His actions are better judged according to the world-view on which they were based.

distinguishes the *dibịa ọgwụ* from the mere herbalist (*dibịa nkpa akwụkwọ*).

Accounts are in good supply of extraordinary episodes in the calling of some *dibịa*. Spirits are said to have taught some of them about herbs and their application (see Appendices1 & 2). These experiences do not, however, offer any *dibịa* the comprehensive knowledge he requires in his profession. He learns about new drugs and treatments as he meets them and this can go on most of the time. Again, the *dibịa* must learn the professional tactics and dispositions for dealing with day to day cases. The *dibịa* always needs to understand the particular circumstance of any case to be able to handle it effectively. This is particularly important in divination. There is the need to complement the supernatural powers of the *dibịa* with the natural and learned skill. Some form of formal learning seem to have always obtained in most societies, for those in charge of the health services. As Waal Malefijt has observed;

> . . . diviners and diagnosticians do not merely rely upon the supernatural for their answers. Often they accompany their magical techniques by shrewd questioning, or by taking their cues from the patient's own suspicions . . . In small communities, where not many things remain hidden the diviner will usually be quite familiar with the personal circumstances of the patients as well as with local antagonism This knowledge will assist him in reaching conclusion which are satisfying to the sufferer and acceptable to the community.[9]

Use of such methods and tactics is common in traditions of *afa* divination. In Urhobo, Nabofa and Elugbe explained:

> There is no doubt that *Epha* priest studies the client's face as he studies the *Epha* patterns. Psychology is therefore probably a strong element in *Epha* consultation. Indeed some skeptics who do not believe in *Epha* insist that the whole process is a psychological exercise during which the *Obuepha* reduces the client to a state of near-hypnosis.[10]

Among the Yoruba, the *Ifa* priest undergoes training which "involves a long and tedious period in the course of which the

---

9   Annemarie de Waal Malefijt, *Religion and Culture: An Introduction to Anthropology of Religion*, Macmillan, New York, 1968, p.254.

10   M.Y. Nabofa and Ben. Elugbe, "Epha: Urhobo System of Divination and its Esoteric Language", p.11

candidate has to master the different techniques, commit to memory a huge amount of the ritual recitations called *odu*."[11]

The common procedure in the training arrangement of the *dibịa* is that a son understudies the father since the profession is inherited. Where this is not possible, in case the father is deceased or has actually not been a practising *dibịa*, an uncle or any other close relation who is a *dibịa* takes over the responsibility. As we have already explained, a break could appear in a family *agwụ* tradition such that there are no living members through whom the tradition is handed over. An aspirant might have to go out of the family to arrange for his training with any *dibịa* of repute.

A young person whose calling has been identified begins early in life to acquire and store the relevant information about the *dibịa* work, the local pharmacopeia and the other substances or objects employed in the preparation of medicine. While in training he accompanies his master when he goes to the bush or forest to get the herbal roots, barks, leaves, fruits and minerals from the wide range of species. Local physicians do not plant elaborate botanical gardens where medicinal herbs grow. However, one or two of such plants may be found growing around the houses of many *dibịa* especially those plants whose parts are put in frequent use. After some years of learning the trainee comes to a stage that he could be sent by the master to collect these medicinal materials.

The candidate in training learns the way different medicinal materials are treated, preserved and used. Right from the start, he is a real assistant who does the more routine and boring jobs, such as crushing dry medicinal barks and other materials into powder as the case may be. He carefully learns which herbs that are decocted with water or wine. He must know at what state of freshness leaves, fruits or minerals have greater medicinal effects.

The trainee who has proved to his master that he has acquired the discipline regarding the confidentiality that should characterize the medical practice is then allowed to be present at consultation sessions when patients are received and their complaints registered. If the *dibi̜a* is healer and diviner, the trainee may learn the techniques of the two practices simultaneously.

The material medicine is considered ineffective until it has been empowered through the rite known as *i̜wake o̜gwu̜*. Varied sacrificial items and forms may be required for different medicines depending on whether a particular medicine is desired to bring about results slowly, swiftly or violently. The trainee must know the details of the rites.

After many years the apprentice learns the rules for administering different medicines. Besides regulations about the dosage, particular medicines have taboos that must be observed for them in order not to neutralize their efficacy. To consume, for example, the medicine called *eze u̜kwu̜ eruala* (the king whose feet never touches the ground), the pot that contains it must not have physical contact with the ground through the period of decoction of the medicine and its application. Those who consume it do so with their feet placed on some elevated foot rest.

There are probing sessions when the comprehension of the trainee is examined. His knowledge of herbs and other medicinal materials, his understanding of the intricate issues about diseases, their causes, their symptoms and his ability to make right judgements with the application of therapies, are subjected to test.

The training of the *dibi̜a* extends to learning and cultivating proper sentiments and attitudes towards *agwu̜* cult symbols and the objects that feature prominently in the professional practice. 'The apprentice', Arinze maintains;

must learn about the *dibia* bag which is very big and deep, with many partitions, and contains all kinds of things. Those who are not *ndi dibia* (i.e., *ndi ofeke*) must not look into the bag . . . [12]

The contents of the bag usually include statuettes or some other symbols of *agwu*, a gourd containing powdered medicine, white chalk, yellow chalk, alligator pepper, pieces of cuttings from medicinal herbs, that are put into frequent use and any other preparations, substances or objects that the *dibia* often uses.

There comes a stage in the training when the apprentice accompanies the master on sick calls and visits. The candidate usually carries the master's *dibia* bag. To be entrusted with this job shows that the candidate has earned the master's trust. The master is convinced that his student would not, even inadvertently, break any taboos pertaining to the bag.

The body of knowledge which a candidate is required to have at the end of his training is extensive. He must possess a very good understanding of the local medicinal herbs, roots, barks, leaves, fruits and most of the local flora that are reputed to have value in the preparation of medicine, as well as poisons and antidotes. The candidate should have learnt about animals, birds, insects, as well as their parts and products and their medicinal uses.

His knowledge extends to the application of such materials as skins, skulls, bones and horns in the treatment of the sick. He is educated to recognize sounds from birds and animals. Some of such sounds are important omens in relation to the fate of a sick person. The trainee must know through such sounds when it is time to give up applying more medicine on a sick person. Birds and animals in the bush are said to see the spirits of dying people and they make such sounds that the *dibia* can well interpret. He is to know about times of the day when medicines are more potent and when their side effects are milder. The apprentice learns in what seasons diseases are more or less responsive to types of treatments.

A diviner-apprentice is expected to comprehend the principles that govern the practice, the application of the tools,

---

12 *Ibid.*

the language of the mediums or the complex divinatory formulae. He must learn to adapt his intonation and to render the divinatory recitations in a way the client should find mystifying. Greater faith and trust in the practices seem to accompany lesser comprehension on the part of clients.

The candidate cultivates a befitting attitude to *ulọ agwụ* (*agwụ* house) and observes how it is furnished. He begins quite early in time to contemplate how to possess one when his training would be over. He would begin already to collect any objects he judges could increase the aura of his *agwụ* house.

Agwụ House (*Ụlo Agwụ*)

The office where the *dibịa* does his work of consultations with patients is the *agwụ* house. This is usually a hut most often set beside the *dibịa*'s main house. Here, he stores his cult and professional paraphernalia, the instruments, tools and materials that he uses in his work. Since it is a place used for divination and invocation of the spirits, it has a deep religious significance. It is a place of encounter with *agwụ* both for the *dibịa* and for the clients. It is spoken of literally as the house where *agwụ* lives.

Agwụ house does not call for any special structural design. What is important is that any place that has been so designated should be furnished, decorated and disguised in such ways that its attributes of sacredness and dreadfulness are made obvious. It is usually protected with taboos and no one enters it except with the express permission of the *dibịa*. Each *dibịa* devotes care and sentiments on it and tries to keep it always in that state that it best reflects a divine presence.

Between one cultural area and the other, marked differences exist in the practice of equipping and furnishing *agwụ* house. Even in the same locality dissimilarities abound. Each *dibịa* is ultimately guided by the revelations he receives from the spirit and his own initiatives and sentiments. This fact is illustrated as we examine the contents of a few *agwụ* houses from different parts of Igboland. That enables us to appreciate the shades of perception that play essential roles in the making of *agwụ* houses.

The contents of *ụlo agwụ* belonging to Nwogu Madugba from Obioma Ngwa of Southern Igboland, besides many minor symbols and tools of work include the following:

Carved Images
Agwụ (The prominent statue of female *agwụ)*
Uke agwụ (A statue of a female attendant)
Nkịta agwụ (The dog)

Symbols
Anya mbele agwụ (Constant *agwụ* watchfulness)
Oke ọfọ (The male *ọfọ)*
Ọfọ agwụ (*Ọfọ* that the *dibịa* has as professional right)
Ọsọnsọ ọfọ (Agent that enhances the operations of *ọfọ)*
Ogu agwụ (The symbol of *agwụ* righteousness)
Ahịajọkụ (The symbol of the god of farm work)

Tools
Abọ agwụ (*Agwụ* ritual basket)
Afa (Divinatory beads tied in four strings)
Akpa agwụ/akpa dibịa (The *dibịa* bag)
Ikpuru mbe (The tortoise shell)
Ogene, kpọkọ kpọkọ, ngbiligba (Gong,rattle,bell, etc.)

In Iselemkpitime, Aniocha of Western Igboland the contents of *ụlọ afa* belonging to Otekenubia Azonuche are far different. Statuettes of *agwụ* do not feature and this is because of the recognition of other local deities as cooperators of *agwụ* in patronizing the *dibịa*. There is here the indication of a less perfect compartmentalization of the deities.

Symbol Objects
Ọkwa chi (A flat wooden board dedicated to *chi)*
Mkpụrụ chi (Seeds dedicated to *chi)*
Ọkpụrụkpụ Nnadi (Wooden board, the symbol of social
                   solidarity)

Ọsịsị (A ritual communication object)

Otolokabi (Elephant tusk)

Ọshọ (A narrow wooden board with a handle which the *dibịa* holds in the hand when solemnly pronouncing curses on evil people)

Tools

Afa (Divinatory medium arranged in four strings)

Kpọkọkpọkọ (Rattle)

Idi (Preparation that compels *afa* to speak the truth)

Agwụ symbols in Odinani Museum shows what does obtain in a typical *ụlọ agwụ* in Nri and its neighbours in northern Igbo area.

Carvings of Agwụ Household

Oke (Husband)

Iyom (Wife)

Okolo (Son)

Agbọghọ (Daughter)

Symbols of Agwụ Attributes

Ụkwụ na ije agwụ (Successful adventure)

Udele agwụ (Power of perception)

Ikenga agwụ (Achieving power)

Ulili agwụ (Precognition)

Nkịta agwụ (The third eye)

Ọfọ agwụ (Authority)

Ikiri (supernatural flying power)

Tools

Agba agwụ (The horn used by the *dibịa* to summon *agwụ* or to make music for it)

Mbe agwụ (Tortoise shell)

Okuku (Gourd used for storing powdered medicine)

Some objects placed in *ụlọ agwụ* are not chosen by convention nor arbitrarily by the *dibịa*. It is explained that the spirit would himself demand that particular objects, carved or moulded be acquired at well determined times. In Ngwa area, the following symbol objects, *nkịta agwụ* (the dog), *abali anọ agwụ* (*agwụ* cosmic force), *abali asatọ agwụ* (*agwụ* full cosmic force) and *okenze agwụ* (central house pillar),[13] are acquired for the *agwụ* house only when the spirit has requested the *dibịa* to do so. It is for the *dibịa* to measure his standing before *agwụ* following *agwụ*'s willingness to grant him the privilege of possessing these symbol objects. To have them is a sign of the good disposition of *agwụ* for the work of the *dibịa*.

The client of the *dibịa* is taken up into a divine milieu as he comes into the *agwụ* house. He feels the looming presence of the supernatural which makes him accept readily the interpretations of divination and with trust the therapies for his ailments.

Agwụ house may be taken in its literal sense as a house for *agwụ*. It is the abode of the many symbols of *agwụ* including the media of divination through which *agwụ* speaks to the diviner. Both the *dibịa* and his client believe that *agwụ* house is a place of meeting of a client who has come to know his fortunes and the god who reveals them through the *dibịa*. It is a type of temple. Its sacredness is so obvious to the *dibịa* who must scrupulously observe certain taboos in order not to incur divine wrath. Before we entered into any *agwụ* house we had to put off our shoes. The episode of Moses in the burning bush in Exodus kept coming to my mind. Often too, photographing was forbidden. Where the *agwụ* house has an inner chamber entry into it is absolutely forbidden to visitors.

The *Afa* Medium

The mediumistic instrument of *afa* divination, the divining beads, are variously called *afa (mkpụrụafa)*, *afa okwe*, *ugiri*, *ogbedega*, *akparata*. The beads are made from the shells of the seeds of the trees *okwe* (lima bean), **ugiri** (native mango) and

---

13   Jona Olo, an informant was so emphatic on the inspiration he received from *agwụ* before he could acquire these objects for his *agwụ* house.

others. A string of *afa* holds four shells. Usually cowries are added to the string in between the shells. Four of the strings are required in *afa* divination. The fall of the *afa* either on the concave or convex side provides the direction of interpretation that constitutes *afa* divination.[14]

The *afa* acquires mediumistic power only after it has been consecrated in the ritual *(igọ afa)*. It is usually a simple ritual consisting of the sacrifice of kola nuts and a fowl. Then, the words of consecration which among other things express the wish that the *afa* commits itself totally to 'speaking' the truth are solemnly pronounced with the consecrator holding *ọfọ* in the hand and tapping it on the ground as a way of tying up issues that are binding on the *afa*. The consecrator rounds off in these or similar words:

Nke ga-agwakwa gị okwu ụgha, (any one that speaks
                                            falsehood)

Ọfọ gbuo kwa ya (may *ọfọ* kill it)
Ọfọ gbuo kwa ya (may *ọfọ* kill it)
Ọfọ gbuo kwa ya (may *ọfọ* kill it)

Here too, the apprehension over the ambivalence of *agwụ* is evident. Earlier ritual control measures notwithstanding, other actions are still considered important, for no actions are superfluous in the bid to restrain *agwụ* from double dealing.

After consecration, the *afa* becomes the medium for *agwụ*.

As Zahan explains:

> The divinatory material thus appears as the middle term or intermediary between the diviner and reality. It is a certain symbolic expression of

---

14   *Afa* divination refers primarily to the system of divination where the *afa* seeds are the major augury instrument. But the term has come to be applied to other forms of divination where such other mediumistic instruments as glass, water etc. are used. In this general application, even necromancy is called *afa*. It appears however, that the earliest form of divination among the Igbo used the *afa* seeds as its proper medium.

reality and as such, can only be utilized by specialists who are intimately acquainted with its exact nature.[15]

A descriptive plaque at Odinani Museum clearly states the function of *afa* as a medium and points out too that other considerations come into the success of divination:

> The doctor-diviner throws his divining chaplets on the ground and by reading the arrangements of the beads facing upwards and downwards he is able to decode *agwu*'s 'secret' information which are believed to be transmitted through the dispositions of the beads which practically are based on the theory of chance and probability. Its validity depends on the process of thinking generated by the doctor-diviner who is expert in interpreting the social and sociopsychological relationships of the society.[16]

The *dibia* virtually speaks to *afa* as though it were a person who is physically present. In Enugu-Ezike, for instance, a diviner's address states:

Akparata. . .
Gere ndi obia anyi na-abia be anyi
Zumeleka, zumeleka nana
Gi zumeleka nana
Zumeleka, zumeleka nana

Akparata . . .
Listen to the visitors that have come to us
Counsel them, counsel them properly
You counsel them properly

---

[15] Dominic Zahan, *The Religion, Spirituality, and Thought of Traditional Africa*, University of Chicago Press, Chicago, 1979, p.86.

[16] Cf. Odinani Museum in Nri, Anambra State, Nigeria. The description of *afa* given on a plaque at the museum states "A chaplet called *(ukpukpa)* is made up of four linked *(ugili)* seeds. Each chaplet is held in each hand and thrown with both hands on the ground simultaneously. Sixteen dispositions are possible. Each disposition has a name.... Each of the dispositions is paired with each other to produce 256 meaningful sentences. Each sentence could be paired with the other to produce 256 * 256 complex sentences and could be paired with others to produce another $256^2 * 256^2$ more compound sentences and so on and so forth." As the description further states, "a good doctor-diviner is one that has a copious memory to remember the meaning and significance of these linked sentences in interpreting human and non-human relationships".

Counsel, counsel them properly

In another instance the divine: thus spoke:

Ogbedega kamalu me mara
Ndi biara fu gi
Ogbedega taa bu gini . . .
Kedu ife i fulu . . .

Ogbedega tell me that I may now those
Who have come to see you.
Ogbedega what is today?
What do you see?

It is held among *agwu* specialists that divination is not quite successful if conducted on the day that is sacred to *agwu*. On *eke*, as it is said in Ngwa area *'agwu adighi acha ezigbo mmama'* (agwu does not display clear messages). The messages are cloudy and difficult to decipher.

In the tradition of *agwu* divination found in parts of Mbaise, it is made quite clear that the reality which is primarily sought and which provides the key to the rest of the mystery is the week day's spirit force. Hence the diviner begins his exercise with the invocation of each day's spirit force:

Ya wuru Eke, ya za Eke
Ya wuru Orie ya za Orie
Ya wuru Afo, ya za Afo
Ya wuru Nkwo, ya za Nkwo

When it is *Eke*, let it answer *Eke*
When it is *Orie*, let it answer *Orie*
When it is *Afo*, let it answer *Afo*
When it is *Nkwo*, let it answer *Nkwo*

When the day's spirit force does not hide its identity then the progress of divination is guaranteed, for it is through linking a client to his proper market spirit force that his origin and identity are revealed, and consequently his problem known. Each

individual is spiritually and socially tied to his or her market, that
is to *Eke, Orie, Afọ* or *Nkwọ.*

Chukwu (God) and other members of the local pantheon are
considered to play important role in *afa* divination. At least they
exercise this role by desisting from subversive designs that could
stall the success of divination. Hence, at the beginning of
divination, the *dibịa* prays to the supreme being.[17]

Chineke ngwa kwuo
Ọ bụ gị kere dibịa
Leriakwụ eleria
Ahụkwala onye nwụrụ anwụ sị ọ dị ndụ
Ahụkwala onye dị ndụ sị ọ nwụọla
Ahụkwala ihe ị na amaghị nga ọ nọ mee gị sa gị na-aka

(God behold
You created the *dibịa*
Scrutinize well
Don't see the dead and say it is alive
Don't see the living and say it is dead
Don't testify in a matter you have not witnessed.)

The *dibịa* believes that ultimately it is God who makes one
dibịa to stand and another to fall. To begin his work a *dibịa*
prays to God for success:

Obasị nọ n'elu, onye okike
Ikechara nkịta, nkịta na-ara nsị, ma gị enye ya eze ọcha
Onye ị wara isi ji ya erie, onye ị wara ọdụ ya, ya erie
Ekwekwala ka m daa

(God above, the creator
You created the dog, the dog eats excreta, but its teeth remain
white

---

17 Prayer recorded at the house of Chief Oparaku Anyanwu from Ekwereazu
Mbaise during an interview session.

You give one man the head of the yam, and another its tail end
Never permit me to fall.)[18]

Both diviners and physicians need the assistance and blessings of ancestors. Quarcoopome has explained that:

the ancestors who first practised medicine or who were past masters and teachers of medicine must be given due honours.[19]

Although *Agwụ* is widely recognized as the patron of the *dibịa*, it is, however, believed that it can work more effectively with the cooperation of the members of the spirit world. The *dibịa* secures this by paying the necessary ritual courtesies such as inviting them to libations or sacrificial communion of kola nuts and white chalk. The Igbo say: *aghụghọ dị na mmụọ dị na mmadụ* (gods are as deceitful as men).

Mediumistic Dreams

There are such dreams that the *dibịa* considers important in relation to his work based on the belief that they bring into communication the worlds of men and spirits and that they are keys to explaining various human physical and psychological conditions. The following categories of dreams are recognized: *nrọ agwụ* (dream induced by *agwụ*), *nrọ ịba* (dream resulting from malaria attack), *nrọ ọrịa* (dream because of any other sickness), *nrọ ike ọgwụgwụ* (dream due to exhaustion) and *nrọ ụkpọrọ* (normal dream). Thus, there are the mediumistic and biophysical explanations to dreams. These types of dreams are qualitatively distinguishable from one another just as their causes are. Malaria for instance, induces frequent and recurrent dreams and with most people they are accompanied by nightmares.

Nrọ agwụ is mediumistic. In it, spirits communicate vital messages to the dreamer or through him to others. Those who

---

18 Prayer recorded during the interview granted by Mishark Uhuohuo Okeoma, at Achara, Uturu.
19 T.N.O. Quarcoopome, *West African Traditional Religion*, African University Press, Ibadan, 1987, p.148.

have the *dibịa* calling may discover it in dreams. Frightful dreams may be necessary to persuade an unwilling person to initiate into the cult. In *nrọ agwụ* the *dibịa* receives information about divination, medicinal substances and their applications. It is well known, says Quarcoopome that:

> traditional doctors often claim that they were taught medicine by the divinities or more generally in dreams or in trances during meetings with spirits in the forest."[20]

Some of our informants claim similar or identical experiences (See Appendices 1 and 2). In the dream, the spirit that is encountered is not always recognized as *agwụ*. Spirits in the forms of children, men, women or some known ancestors have been identified. In dreams, ancestors continue to teach their successors about herbs and their applications.[21] They do this to promote the work of their progenies and to keep the tradition alive among the living members of their family. A renowned *dibịa* is expected, after his death, to go on transmitting part of his knowledge to future generations through dreams.

Agwụ and Other Human Values

The highly diffused state of the *agwụ* force has been illustrated by preceding treatments by which it has been shown that the existence of some social institutions and practices are underpinned by the *agwụ* dogma. The *agwụ* force is exceedingly valued in the pursuit and realization of familial values. The onomastic evidence of the impact of *agwụ* shows how deeply it penetrates the understanding of human fate and survival. *Agwụ* cult practices also strengthen the social bonds of agnate and enate families through the belief that *agwụ* possession is derived from both sources.

---

20 *Ibid.*
21 Oparaku Anyanwu, an informant and a renowned *dibịa* claims to receive such tutorials twenty four years after his father had died. He admits however, that the revelations in the dreams usually occur when he is confronted with unfamiliar or very difficult cases.

Perfection of the mind was in the ancient Igbo society recognized as property of the *Omenka/Qmeoka* (the artist). *Agwu* is believed to endow the *Okpuebo* (wood sculptor) with knowledge of supernatural figures that he represents on wood. Craftsmen and blacksmiths who manifest lots of creativeness in their work do so because they are inspired by *agwu*. Some who show great talents in singing and dancing and in other areas of artistic expressions have *agwu* as patron spirit. *Agwu*, as Odoemene said:, "selects . . . men and women for the highest jobs in the society."[22] *Agwu* is respected as the animator of the human mind, as the great source of knowledge especially of the mysteries of the supernatural world. It is a dynamic spirit that brings about development of human perfections such as oratory *(onuohaeshe or ire),* valour *(okpompi)* and influence *(anya ka anya).*[23] It blesses people with *oprum* (success), *ukwu na ije* (successful adventures) and *mbata aku* (wealth). The aspirant must obtain the symbol of the desired value and have it consecrated by the *dibia.* He then takes it home and empowers it regularly with sacrifices as directed.

---

22   Nnamdi Anacletus Odoemene, "African Worldview and Experience of the Holy Spirit" *Bigard Theological Studies* (Jan - June 1994, Vol. 14 No.1):30.

23   *Onuoha(eshe),* literally means public mouth. *Ire* means tongue. The orator is one who speaks with public mouth or public tongue because he speaks in a way that moves the public or in a way the public wants the thing said. He is the one who speaks with the tongue of *agwu* for it is only with its inspiration that one so speaks. *Okpompi* has horns with which it fights. It gives the possessor the courage to face the enemy and fight rather than flee. *Anya ka anya* literally means one whose eyes overpower those of others. An influential person has the overpowering eyes or personality.

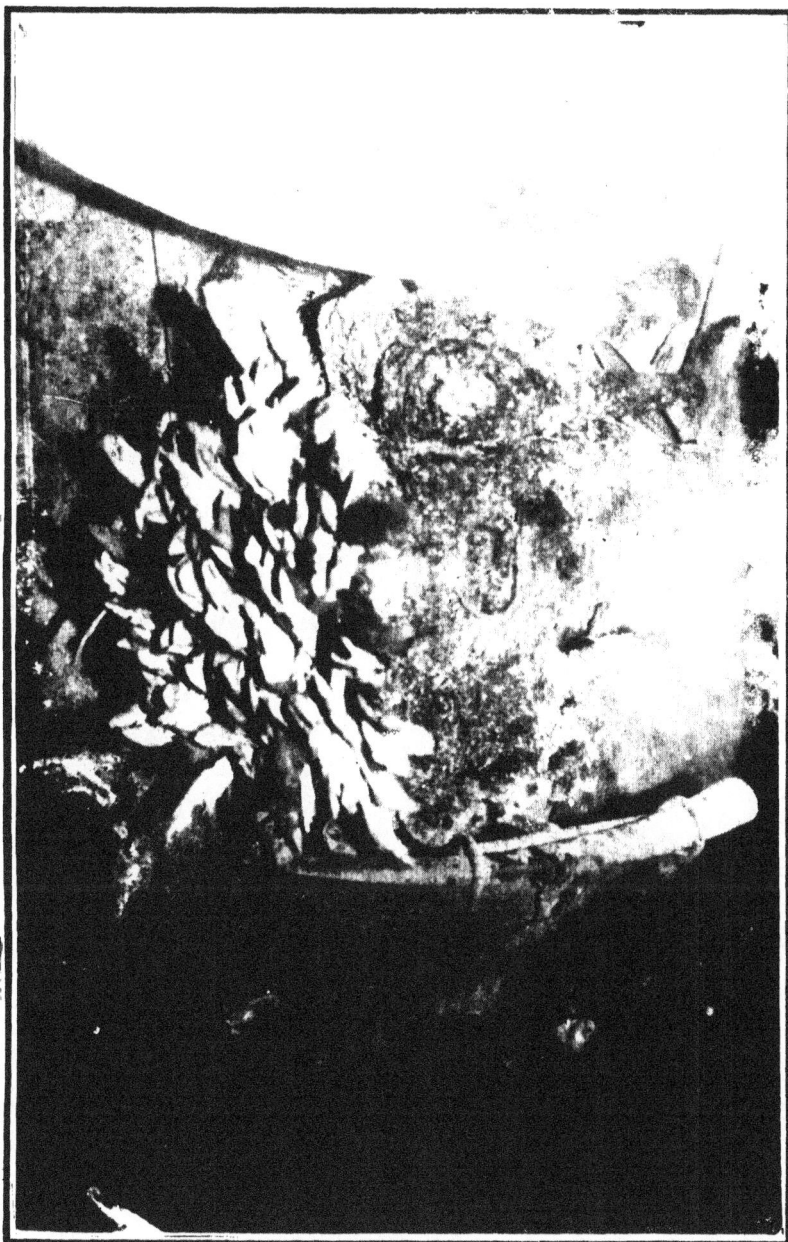

Shrine inside agwụ house at Enugu-Ezike

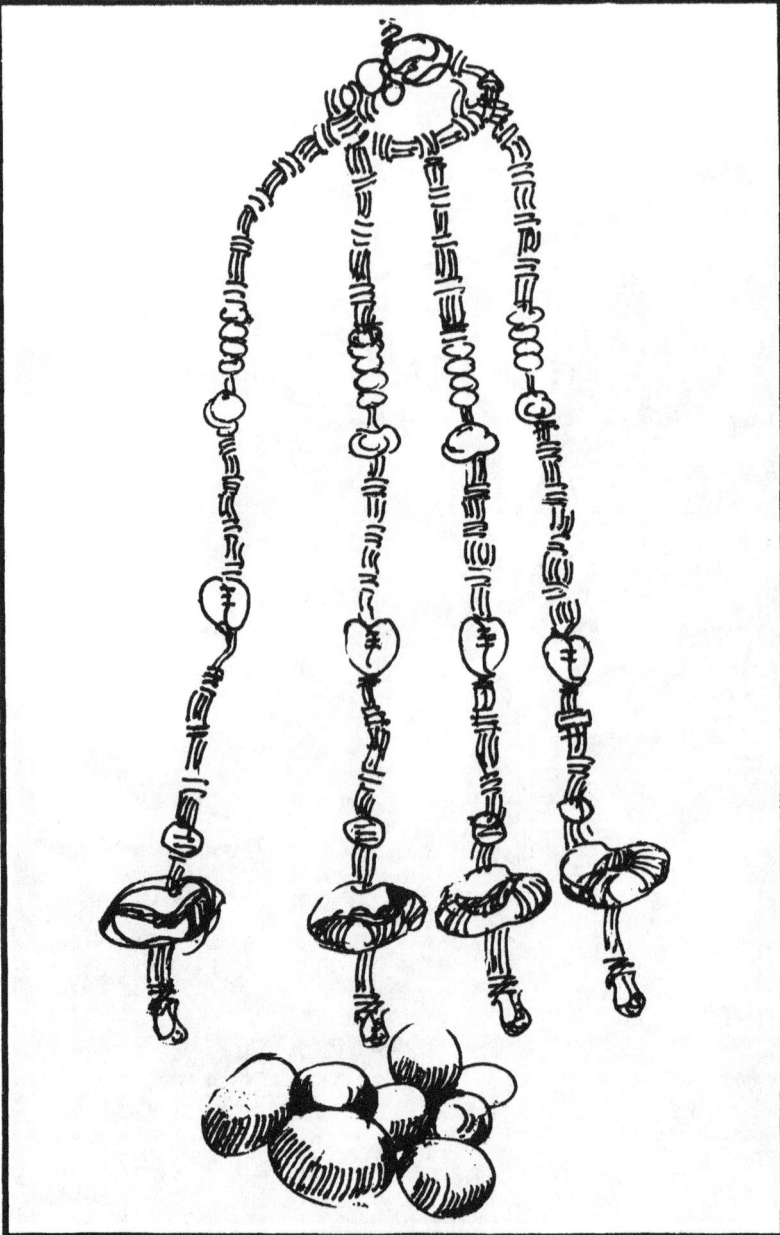

Afa beads

Chapter 6

A g w ụ Therapeutic Force in Time Perspective

Change and Persistence in the Igbo Traditional Culture

Contact with European culture and Christianity has caused visible transformations in the social and cultural institutions of Africa. For most Africans, however, life has not been simply a matter of choosing the new values and abandoning the indigenous ones or vice versa. There have been tensions, dilemmas, uncertainties and even confusion concerning preference of either the traditional or European cultural institutions. The visible consequence is that Africans have assimilated a lot of the foreign culture, and have thereby sacrificed equally, a lot of their indigenous culture.

Despite the obvious transformations as evidenced by big cities and housing complexes, industries and amazing structures, an enduring perplexity with the identity crisis which many Africans have exhibited has kept alive the arguments on issues of the destruction of African culture and its revival. The arguments have meant that from time to time, stock is taken of the indigenous culture, how much is destroyed and modified and how much is retained even as the process of acculturation continues.

It can be firmly said that the impact of Western Culture and Christianity on the Igbo traditional religion, as enormous as it may appear, has not eroded all allegiance to the Igbo traditional religion. This is because the answers to human suffering, fears, anxieties, and other crisis that the traditional religion has fashioned for many centuries are so deeply entrenched that they are not easily replaced even by those of Christianity or the modern systems. Although Christianity appears to have displaced the traditional religion, the latter still commands the loyalty of many. Such loyalty, even in recent times has been found, not only to exist, but to be strong. In 1986 Ejizu had noted;

> No doubt, Igbo traditional religion is down, but not out in contemporary Igbo religious scene. In spite of the devastating effect of Christianity and western culture and civilization, the traditional religious culture is far from being an anachronism. Rather, it continues to be the potential factor and a living institution for a faithful remnant in the system.[1]

About the same period, the Catholic bishops of Southern Nigeria warned of the danger of a light coating of Christianity which succeeds in hiding continued respect and acceptance of the traditional religion and its practices. In a pastoral letter they remarked;

> Christianity has made impact in our society, there has been real increase in numbers. Some discernible changes have been made in the personalities of many people due to Christianity but the extent of such changes must not be exaggerated. There is abundant evidence to show the prevalence of superstitious native customs and beliefs as well as materialism under a thin veneer of Christianity among many of our Christians.[2]

---

1   C. Ejizu, "Continuity and Discontinuity in Igbo Traditional Religion". In Emefie Ikenga-Metuh, (Ed.) *The Gods In Retreat: Continuity and Change In African Religions*, Fourth Dimension Publishers, Enugu, 1986, pp.148-149. In this same passage, Ejizu firmly notes that the traditional religion is very much intact and thrives in such areas as Abakaliki, Afikpo, Awka, Awgu, Ngwa, Oji, Udi, and Ogbaru districts. In these areas he observes, "Igbo traditional religious beliefs and practices, still thrive in much the same way as in the period that could be referred to as the golden age of the Igbo traditional culture, notwithstanding the presence of Christian religion in these areas." Recently, my intervention became necessary in order that a woman, from Lokpanta, whose husband had just died should be exempted from undergoing a gruesome traditional rite of mourning. The woman and her deceased husband were christians, well married in Church and practising. The relatives of the dead man, who are also Christians had intended to impose the rite on her. This situation occurs quite often and is indicative of the continuing impact of the traditional religious world-view.

2   Bishops of Onitsha Ecclesiastical Province, "Put out into deep waters". A pastoral letter on the first Centinary celebration of the Advent of the Catholic Church in Eastern Nigeria, Onitsha, 1986, pp.11-12.

Similar observation by Ikenga-Metuh reveals facts which confirm that devotion to the indigenous religion has remained not simply a matter for some distraught remnant. On the contrary, there is significant participation even by avowed Christians;

> In Nigeria, belief in *ọgbanje* or *abiku* (evil spirits which reincarnate repeatedly in children) are still firmly held. Rituals to exorcise them are openly made by Christians and traditionalists, the educated and the uneducated alike. Consultation of oracles and divination are widely practised especially to discover causes of the death of relatives, causes of illness, and to identify thieves, witches and sorcerers.[3]

Today, evidence of the resilience of the indigenous religion is seen in the many instances of conflict, involving traditional religionists, cultural revivalists and other members of the community especially Christians. While changes go on, the effort by many to protect and promote socio-cultural practices is open and persistent. For example, there are traditional institutions such as *Ọzọ, Ọkọnkọ, Odo* and *Mmọnwụ,* over which Christians and traditionalists have had little agreement in the dialogue to discover if their elements are irreconcilably opposed. There are still other personal and social crises arising from preferences of values of either the Western or the traditional systems. Change continues but manifests features of the recrudescence of traditional practices. It is indeed the view of many Africanist writers that, since many African values are deep-seated and have proved to be vital to Africans, intercultural dialogue conducted without prejudice and undue aggression might prove the only viable way for modernization and authentic

---

3   Emefie Ikenga-Metuh, *Comparative Studies of African Traditional Religion,* IMICO Publishers, Onitsha (Nigeria), 1987, p.272. One finds Sylvia Leith-Ross being echoed in Metuh, forty-eight years after she described the state of Christian practice in Igboland. In her account, "An Igbo attends communion at the same time as he believes in the potency of traditional magic; he ties up in the same handkerchief the rosary and the traditional talisman and plants side by side in the garden round his new cement and pan-roofed house the hibiscus of civilization and the *ogirisi* tree of pagan family rites." Cf. *African Woman* (1939), Routledge and Kegan Paul, (1965), p.239.

development in Africa. Camps Arnulf's view in 1976 is still a valid advice for such a project;

> ... I would like to stress the fact that we should not think that the African outlook described above will disappear with modernization, urbanization, and so forth. It now seems quite clear to me that we are dealing here with categories and themes that go very deep. At times they may change their outer forms or even become shapeless, but they will never disappear from the African heart. In the past we have spoken all too negatively about them, and we have acted thoughtlessly in our efforts to uproot them. One clear consequence has been the rise of independent churches, since Africans did not feel that they were understood by western Christianity. These splinter movements of varying size and importance now number well over six thousand, and the figure is still growing.[4]

As a result of the religio-cultural transformations, *agwụ* cult practices have undergone some modifications that have also made them even more compatible with contemporary sensitivity. The services of *agwụ* specialists, especially, those of the diviner and the physician, have been sought for, as needs of people arise irrespective of religious affiliations. Some people who have officially renounced the traditional religion discover the need to go back to it in the face of certain problems they find to be intractable. At some stage in their search for solutions, they are easily drawn to agreeing with the opinion that such problems are only effectively managed through 'traditional means'. It is not only the rural dwellers but also the elites of the new communities of urban cities, who seek the services of the *dibịa*. As Ikenga-Metuh has said;

> Their clientele thus cuts across the old and new ethnic, social and religious groupings. This is borne out by the scores of sign boards in different Igbo cities, and the many advertisements in the newspaper.[5]

The daily record of consultations differ from *dibịa* to *dibịa* and from one locality to another. While Ali Nweke of Ogrute Ulo in Enugu-Ezike for example, has an average of three

---

4   Camps Arnulf, *Partners in Dialogue*, Orbis Books, Maryknoll, (New York), 1983, p.119.

5   Emefie Ikenga-Metuh, *African Religions in Western Conceptual Schemes: The Problem of Interpretation*, Pastoral Institute, Bodija, Ibadan, 1985, p. 167.

consultations a day, Oparaku Anyanwu of Ekwereazu Mbaise records as many as fifteen. Factors such as, the reputation of the *dibia*, the given population in a locality, the state of the indigenous religion, and the number of practitioners, are decisive to the size of clientele which any *dibia* might have. During the several times we visited Chief Oparaku Anyanwu, we always met many people waiting to consult him. In fact, on two occasions he was so busy attending to patients that we had to take new appointments.

In some other instances, traditional doctors erect accommodations and admit patients. Agwu Okuonu of Ekoli Edda has a ward where patients with mental illness are admitted and cured. As many as twelve patients were in admission in his clinic at the time of our visit. Many of the *dibia* are young, pragmatic and resourceful and easily exercise the knack for giving modern touch to their practices. Their institution seems well set in place to survive the currents of change for still a long time.

Those who consult the *dibia*, including the Christians, do so convinced of the efficacy of the indigenous institutions. Some simply assert that Christianity cannot provide satisfactory explanation and solution to the many traumas of their lives, for there are such human problems, often life-threatening, that are so deep and mysterious which are better kept outside the jurisdiction of Christianity if ever one would master them. The experience of a Catholic nun, a researcher, who had come to interview Chief Anyanwu is a demonstration of the wide acceptance of this view. According to the nun, she overheard a brief exchange between two women who were waiting for their turns outside Chief Oparaku Anyanwu's consultation room. One had asked the other if nuns also have the need to consult the *dibia*. The other replied that they certainly do have, for they too, are human beings.

The problems for which Christians consult the *dibia* are those believed to arise as a result of attacks by spirits and their agents, and in that case they accept as appropriate means of dealing with them, the well known provisions of the traditional institutions. Such provisions include rituals of atonement. They are means that have been developed, tried and that have flourished for a very long period, as part of the traditional religious system.

Christians accept that these spirits exist and the teaching of Christianity is not silent on spirits that are malevolent and antagonistic to man. The traditional religion, however, is believed by many, to have a more realistic and effective way of dealing with them. In recent times the great success of the many Christian healing homes in Africa is accounted for by their claims to provide more effective means of coping with evil spirits and their agents.

Religious Therapeutic Institutions in contemporary Igbo Society

Traditional health institutions of Igbo society have retained their popularity up to the present time. Besides other reasons that account for this, there is often, among traditional healers, the effort to combat what they regard as the menace of modern orthodox medicine and that of Christian Healing Ministries. This attempt is not always subtle but open. Its result is the division of diseases made by some *dibịa,* between those that cannot be handled by modern medicine and those that can only be treated by traditional medicine. Christian based practices of religious therapy have also become quite numerous. Ministries of the main Christian Churches, sects, charismatic groups and indigenous Christian Churches offer one form of therapy or the other.

Some of these are likely to admit the power of orthodox medicine but make such power dependent on the divine will. As one tries to understand the various institutions of health and the influences they exert on each other, several factors which account for the enduring appeal of religious therapy, whether the traditional or Christian-based, emerge. As we examine these factors it becomes clear that they are tied to issues which the people concerned regard with the highest importance. The result then is the continued relevance of the religious therapeutic institutions.

Underdevelopment

Since urban and rural areas fundamentally differ on grounds of modernization levels, traditional practices maintain greater virility in the latter. The traditional world-view, and the traditional structures and institutions have remained much more intact in the rural areas. Western education in many rural areas has been limited in its contribution to social transformation and development because of the poor school facilities turning out people who are mere half literate. High urban migrations are signs of the greater opportunities that exist there.

What the rural area means in view of health services is that modern medical institutions and facilities are found absent or highly inadequate. In most cases, government medical institutions are in such bad conditions regarding staff and equipment that they have remained to serve the inverse role of symbols of neglect. Generally, in the less developed parts of Igboland, the *dibia* has remained the most reliable and available source of relief in cases of sickness and other misfortunes.

In such areas, the twilight of the traditional profession is still some good way off and may remain so until effective modern medical facilities become available. But even when that happens, there is the question of the high cost of medical services and drugs that is out of proportion with the wealth of the rural dwellers. In recent times, government programmes have focused on rural health services. Health programs sponsored by international bodies, such as the World Health Organization or the United Nations Children's Fund, are having some visible impact. Such efforts increasingly contribute in bringing greater development to the rural areas and providing the needed alternatives of health care to the dwellers.

Some Similarities in Health Service Practices

Some doctrines and practices of Christian religion are similar to those of traditional religion. A typical example question of disease causation where both religions express b in disease causing spirits and spirit agents. In traditional relig ., there are *agwu, akalogoli* (evil spirits), spirits of relatives that are denied funerary rites, deities whose taboos have been infringed, and the *ọgbanje* that afflict children. These cause effects similar to those attributed to the devil, demons or evil spirits, who according to Christian belief, can cause sickness, misfortune and human suffering when they possess human beings.

The *dibịa* and the Christian religious healer apparently fight common human enemies. Both strive to accomplish human liberation from disease and its spirit agents. The table below presents some clear picture of the situation.

Some traditional and Christian health service practices

	Christianity	Traditional Religion
Causes of sickness (except natural causes)	The devil, demons, evil spirits.	Bad spirits *(akalogoli)*, spirits of the dead, sorcerers, witchcraft.
Types of sickness	Biological, mental, possession by evil spirits.	Biological, mental, possession by spirits.
Specialists	The priest, the prophet healer, the spiritual healer etc.	The *dibịa* (priest, diviner and physician)
Healing methods	Confession of offence, prayers, fasting, apply hospital treatment.	Confession and sacrifice to remove divine wrath, remove sorcerous objects, offer sacrifices, apply medication.
Protective rituals, preventives.	Place blessed sticker on the door to the home; use other Christian symbols, eg the cross or miraclous medals, burn candles and incense; use specially blessed creams and soap on the body; use holy water; identify and expose disease causing objects planted by enemies.	Use of *ẹkike* (protective preparation, amulets, charms, talisman) , order for the ritual of *ịgbusi ahụ* (fortifying the body), plant around the house spirit-scaring shrubs, use other spirit-repellents.

These similarities as the table shows, explain the possibility of the increasingly eclectic tendency, by which many accept simultaneously or consecutively, the mediation of the *dibịa*, the modern doctor and the Christian healing minister. Of course, it is generally true that in a desperate case one is likely to accept whatever means that appear to hold some promise of relief, sometimes in deliberate defiance to one's particular religious faith. A Christian, who has found the traditional method effective, is most unlikely to condemn it. Fr. Goddy Ikobi, well known in the Christian healing ministry circle, has clearly stated this experience;

> In general, when an average Nigerian Christian falls sick, he either goes to hospital or goes to the native doctor. If he is cured, the problem stops there, but if he is not cured, he may switch over from the hospital to the native doctor or from the native doctor to the hospital or in some cases he goes straight to the oracle. If at the end, all these efforts fail, he turns to the prayer houses. It is at this stage that I usually come in contact with most of them.[6]

The many religious therapists of the Christian Churches, who combine herbal medicine and Christian prayers, and they are not only from the Christian sects but also from main line Churches, such as the Catholic Church or the Anglican Church, have contributed in very significant ways to the persistence and increasing popularity of the traditional healing practice.[7] They do so through the liberal sharing of elements. With growing easy combination of Christian and traditional healing elements and

---

6   Goddy Ikobi, "Healing and Exorcism: The Nigerian Pastoral Experience'. In Chris U. Manus, Luke N. Mbefo and E.E. Uzukwu (Eds.) *Healing And Exorcism: The Nigerian Experience*, Spiritan International School of Theology, Attakwu- Enugu, 1992, p.60.

7   Sanneh has described the distinctive African Spirituality such as practised in the healing churches to consist in combining "the two fundamental elements of Christianity and African culture in a way that advertises their Christian intention without devaluing their African credentials." Cf., L. Sanneh, *West African Christianity: Religious Impact*, Orbis Books, Maryknoll, New York, 1983, p.180. Much earlier Adrian Hastings noted that the Christian healing practices in the Healing Houses are informed by traditional perceptions of healing. "They do not for a moment deny the presence of spirits to be cast out, witchcraft spells to be housed, but faced with them they assert the power of God to free and to restore. In practice there seems to be a wide range of response, at one end clearly controlled by a Christian sense of God and Christ; at the other it is still rather deeply embedded in the religious metaphysics underlying traditional treatment." Cf., *African Christianity*, Geoffrey Chapman, London, 1976, p.72

methods, any differences between the two are more and more obscured.

Eclectic Tendencies of Traditional Religionists

Specialists of *agwu* cult have become very innovative and are establishing linkages between the *agwu* dogma and those of Judaism and Christianity. All these religions accept the idea of a creator, God, to whom all other creatures owe their existence. In recent times protagonists of the *agwu* cult have gone further to make claims to historical and dogmatic affinities with the Middle East and its religions. There has consequently emerged strong dogmatic syncretism which seems all the while to benefit the *agwu* cult. We shall clarify this situation with three examples based on our research.

Agwu specialist, John Chima Ama of Edda links the discovery of *agwu* to the Red Sea episode, when Moses parted the sea so that the Israelites might walk across on dry ground. The Igbo people are Jews he affirms. As they crossed the red sea, they found two stones on the sea bed. One stone was *agwuisi* and the other was *kamalu* (god of thunder and lightning). Ama traces a confusing route of migration from Egypt to Edda in Abia State of Nigeria.

He claims that the Edda initiation rite, which is still in use, and called *egbela ndi juu* (Jew) owes its origin to the ancestral Jewish culture. This view is also shared by some other people of Edda. The stone, *agwu,* which was picked up from the Red Sea according to Ama, had the shape of a bowl and it had served the migrants as cooking utensil when they first settled in Edda.[8]

---

8   Anthropological studies have so far failed to establish satisfactory evidence of a linkage of the Igbo people to the Jewish race. In the article, "The Traditions of Origin", Professor A.E. Afigbo reviewed the suggestions of Igbo oriental origin by such authors as Olaudah Equiano (1789), G.T. Basden (1912), Ike Akwaelumo (c.1950). He considers the oriental theory the least of the most relevant theories in the study of Igbo origin and his final evaluation of the theory is that "it is worthless as an account of Igbo origin,... Not only is there no concrete evidence in its support, but it is in conflict with what concrete archaeological and linguistic evidence we have."

Ama makes an analogical correlation of the staff of Moses and *ọgwụ*. The staff that at God's behest turned to a serpent (Exodus 4: 1-5) was a gift of miraculous power from God. *Agwụ* patronizes *ọgwụ* (medicine) and the latter, like the staff of Moses, is miraculous power from God.

Ama finds in the relationship of God and the prophets of the Old Testament, a good parallel to that of the diviner and *agwụ*. Moses was a seer and when he came down from Mountain Sinai after meeting Yahweh, the skin of his face was radiant and the people did not dare to approach him (Exodus 34:29-31). The diviner in his work makes spiritual journey to the world of the gods to receive messages. The abnormal characteristics the *dibịa* manifest are the signs of the intimate contact they have with the divine beings.

The Oriental theories by which some ethnic groups of Africa link their origin to the Middle East is very much diffused such that they have been assumed as intelligible bases for the reconstructive modification of practices in the traditional religion. The appeal of these theories to a protagonist of such project, such as Ama, who has but the most elementary acquaintance with accounts of biblical episodes, reveals, among other things, the anxiety underlying a determination to find other and more acceptable foundations for the indigenous practices, in order to make them still widely acceptable.

Our second example is based on the views of Uwakwe Onyeakobusi, an *agwụ* devotee, who identified *agwụ* with Jesus Christ. For many who have found Jesus Christ, a

---

(Cf. "Traditions of Igbo origin:A comment", *Nigeria Magazine*, No. 144, 1983,p.3ff.) But the propagation of the theory has received a boost from private religious experiences which are propagated as divine revelations. There are such revelations made to the stigmatist, Innocent Okorie of Owerri-Ebiri in Orlu Local Government Area of Imo State. Some of his "followers" have accepted these revelations as authentic. For instance, it is on that basis that Dr. Ezeala, an author, offers a proof of Igbo-Jewish origin. He even took over the title of *Jabborigbo*, the revealed name of the leader of the *Schechenigbo* (Igbo) during their flight from Israel to escape the Assyrian persecution. (Cf. J.O.J. Ezeala, *The Great Debate*, B.I. Nnaji & Sons Press, Orlu 1992.)

paradox, likening him to the ambivalent *agwụ* would seem a fair calculation. According to Uwakwe, Jesus Christ is the son of God who found him to be self-willed and intransigent and on that account drove him out of heaven into the world. While on earth, he persisted in his character and came into conflict practically with everyone in his society including political leaders who had to put him to death. Uwakwe concluded that in coming into the world, Jesus is *agwụ* and is accountable for many human problems.

Uwakwe who did not receive formal education and generally showed fragmented comprehension of bible stories could be mixing up the popularly known account of Satan and Michael, where the former was driven down from heaven (Revelation 12:7-9).[9] This might also be a case of an ingenious attempt to provide such validation for beliefs and practices of the traditional religion that renders them more appealing to contemporary taste. Its success could actually represent the fulfillment of the dreams increasingly shared by many traditional religionists that their religious world-view become translatable into Christian religious ideas. When that succeeds, then would it also widen the scope of pervasive syncretism.

The third example is the situation of increasing eclectic approach, by which traditional religionists invoke the Christian God in their prayers. It quite often happens that traditional religionists when saying public prayers end them as Christians do with 'Through Christ our Lord' or begin such prayers with a trinitarian formula. Many explanations are given for this development. It is seen by some as the effect of close contact between the followers of both religions - just a matter of unconscious response to influences. The development is seen also as the result of the tendency of the traditional religionists to

---

9 The story of Michael and Satan says: "And now war broke out in heaven, when Michael with his angels attacked the dragon. The dragon fought back with his angels, but they were defeated and driven out of heaven. The great dragon, the primeval serpent, known as the devil or Satan, who had deceived the world, was hurled down to the earth and his angels were hurled down with him (Rev. 12:7-9, *The Jerusalem Bible*, School Edition).

invoke, in their rituals, all known sources and centres of power.[10]

Some still explain this as a reflection of the religious liberalism that is characteristic of the Igbo people. It might also be realistic to think of the courtesy of the traditional practitioner who would not like to offend some members of an audience by the use of exclusive prayers. But when a *dibịa* does the same in his *agwụ* house, where he has no need to show tolerance or flexibility at the expense of orthodoxy, then more serious motives are likely to be present. As we entered Madugba's *agwụ* house, all the paraphernalia of the cult were arranged in their positions. He welcomed us and while pouring libations of wine, he prayed:

Chineke nna, Chineke ọkpara, Chineke mụọ nsọ
Eze onye akụ na ọgwụ dị n'aka
Onye mere ọbara mee miri
Onye ma mkpa ụmụ ogbenye
Ọgwọ mgbe ike gwụrụ dibịa
Agịga e ji tọọ ihe mara akpụ

Nna anyị Madugba hụkwa manyị ñụrụ

Ala ñụrụ manyị

Ndịche Nwoke ñụrụ manyị

Ndịche nwanyị ñụrụ manyị

Ọ dị ihe ha si we bịa gbuo
Ma ọ bụ ije ọma ya dịrị ha mma
Ihe ha chọrọ rukwe ha aka
Ihe ọma mere ha, nke ọjọọ gbaa
Ha bịa ije ọjọọ, ya adịrịlị ha mma

---

10 Nwoga has observed that "while we may be laughing at the non-christian villager who concludes his kola prayer with: *N'aha Jesu Christi Onye nwe anyị* (Through Christ Our Lord), the villager is engaged in the serious business of saving himself from blame and punishment by accommodating a new and obviously strong deity brought by the missionaries." (Donatus I.Nwoga, 1984 Ahịajọku Lecture, p.43).

Enwere m nwanyị agwụ
Enwere m nkịta agwụ
Enwere m anya mbelelu agwụ
Ihe dị ọtụtụ
Agaghị agba aka agbafu ntị
Enwere m ihinjọkụ, enwere m oke ọfọ
Enwere m uke agwụ, nwoke agwụ, nwanyị agwụ

Ndị a bịara ijụ ihe ha na amaghị
Ya gara ha nke ọma
N'aha Kristi

Ihe madụ na-amaghị madụ je ezi ya
O nwekwanịrị ihe dị mkpa dị n'ime -
Ọ bụ ahụkata nwoke agaghị ahụkwa ya

Nwa a bịara mmụta
E nwee ihe o na-eje ma ọ bụ ọrụ a ga-iji arụ
Ma ọ bụ akwụkwọ o je ịgụ agụ
Ma ọ bụ ije ọ ga-ịga aga
Ma ọ bụ ọ ga-iji ịchọ ikpeghe
Ya dịkwara ya mma-
N'aha Kristi
Mma mma nụ, mma mma nụ

(God the father, God the son, God the holy spirit
King in whose hand are wealth and healing
Who made blood, made water
Who knows the needs of the poor
Who heals when the *dibịa* has given up
You, the needle with which the knot is untied

Our father Madugba, here is wine to drink
Earth, drink wine
Male ancestors, drink wine
Female ancestors, drink wine

They (visitors) have come for a purpose
If for good, may it go well with them
May they find what they seek

May what is good be theirs, may evil flee
If for evil, may it not go well with them

I have female *agwụ*
I have *nkịta agwụ*
I have *anya mbelelu agwụ*
The things are many
No one bores a hole in the ear barehanded
I have *Ihinjọkụ*, I have *oke ọfọ*
I have *uke agwụ*, male *agwụ* and female *agwụ*

These have come to ask about what they do not know
May it go well with them
In the name of Christ

What one does not know another shows him
But there is that which is critical that happens-
That man is there [in the world] for a time and is seen no
more

This man has come to learn
If he will go anywhere or will use it to work
Or for the purpose of studies
Or for some venture
May it go well with him
In the name of Christ)
You are welcome, you are welcome.

In this short prayer preceding the interview session,
Madugba used the trinitarian formula once and the Christ
formula twice. He did so with almost customary familiarity as
though these divine persons had always been members of the
traditional pantheon. Some *dibịa* in contemporary times have
made themselves and their services more acceptable after they
have at first deceived the clients into believing they are Christians
for they display Christian symbols and recite Christian prayers.

Hawkers of religious therapy from unpopular Christian sects
adopt the same strategy for they purposely pretend to be in

communion with the main line Christian Churches to earn undeserved credibility. Such motives might be ascribed to Nwogu Madugba and others who have resorted to the use of popular Christian formulae of which they have little or no comprehension but whose function they well appreciate.[11]

Adaptation of Indigenous Religious Practices

The involvement of Christians in *agwụ* has been encouraged by the flexibility which has become applicable in the use of initiation rites in order to satisfy the special circumstances of Christians, elites and those who live in urban areas. Christians are afraid of being publicly denounced as double-faced and of endangering their membership in their churches. The elite group has to pretend that the traditional rituals of initiation do not appeal to its civilized taste. Urban areas do not also afford the environment required for elaborate rituals. People in these groups can be secretly initiated with minimum rites. Money is paid as substitute for omitted rites. Those concerned are allowed to keep just the simplest cult symbols should they find the normal sizes cumbersome. With such possibilities available, people who have the need conveniently and privately settle issues with *agwụ*.

Countering New Forms of Insecurities

Many indications confirm that on the whole religiosity is on the increase in Africa. There have been revival groups in the moslem religion and in the Christian religion innumerable sects attest to a complex religious development.

Sociological studies on the subject of increasing sects have discovered many reasons. One prominent reason in the present times is the question of health. Many people, including Christians, are easily overcome by those evasive problems of

---

[11] When one goes on to analyze this prayer in view of exposing its reflection of the nature of the traditional religion and principal views on *agwụ* one sees two important points. The first is the prayerful attitude shown towards God and the ancestors. They transcend man and the latter accepts their authority as sovereign. The second point is that *agwụ* is talked of as a property of man. Madugba has *agwụ* of all types'. This points to the anthropocentirc doctrine on *agwụ* by which it is a spriit that depends on human persons for its manifestation and propagation in the world.

life, especially when they pertain to health and threaten life. The efforts of the faith healing churches or prayer houses to contend them are not often rewarded with success and further search for solution often leads by way of a U-Turn to traditional religious means.

Another important reason arises from the complex social and political changes. This is the period of experiments with new political, economic and social systems which have created unfamiliar forms of insecurities. Some people who are affected find indigenous religious remedies viable recourse as they seek protection in charms and 'medicines'. If reports in the newspapers are anything to go by, then the medicine-man is alive and active in political rallies, in parliament, offices, universities and even in the football field.

The politicians who might be Christians distribute money to voters along with oath on some dreaded *arusị* (deity) as a way of securing their support. There is 'medicine' to influence a bill in parliament and there is 'medicine' for protection against jealous political opponents. Some of the elite group still believe that even little chances of good fortune have to be induced with medicine.

The breakdown of traditional social securities, the indiscipline of the emerging society and the proliferation of social ills particularly armed robbery, have created a high level of insecurity, making *ọgwụ* a type of emergency exit. As the law enforcement agencies seem to have been justly discredited as unreliable and inefficient, 'medicine' is looked up to as an alternative means of protection. The resourcefulness of the *dibịa* may have been highly overstretched. He prepares *ekike* (amulets) for warding off armed robbers or for confusing them when they threaten; for recovering property when already stolen; for guarding people and their homes; for helping to detect fraud etc. In divination, the *dibịa* unveils the identities of thieves, sorcerers and witches, opponents and enemies, and tells a man about his fortune, and perhaps precisely, what fortune a particular journey holds in stock for him.

In traditional society *ǫgwụ,* (medicine) is power and this realization has persisted in many a contemporary man. During my interview in Edda, a *dibịa* offered to prepare medicine of good luck for me, and a special one for that matter - "one that a woman could not even neutralize". That would have been an attractive offer to a desperate politician or businessman or a man with many enemies. The situation of insecurities to which modern institutions provide no answers, means that for quite some time still, the *dibịa* will continue to be relevant in African society.

The Economic Factor

The economic value of the traditional medical profession was a major reason of the attraction it has held for many over the years.The charges and shares of flesh of victims used at health rituals made the *dibịa* much more comfortable than many of his neighbours.

We know from examining some myths of *agwụ* origin that families where *agwụ* force exist, which is expressed in the form of gaining mastery over some skill, sought to maintain monopoly over such skill. The whole idea is to keep within the family a viable source of income. Most *dibịa* are inclined to retain monopoly in the work because they see it simply as a means of livelihood. Some guard their secrets scrupulously so that they would have few competitors in their areas of expertise. One such *dibịa* had explained to me:

> The work I do as *dibịa* is a gift which has immense value particularly regarding my livelihood and I try to see that it does not become a trade that is offered to other bidders. I also feel it would be irresponsibility on my part to do otherwise. God gave me this gift. His purpose was to give me a means of survival. He could give it also to any one of his choice. I have nothing against that. But the one given to me I must hold and protect.[12]

Today, reputable traditional physicians and diviners belong to the class of the well-to-do in their societies. That has drawn

---

12   Ali Nwaeke, oral interview. It is remarkable that Ali learnt medicine and divination directly from the spirits. He was never an apprentice to anyone and has not allowed anyone to be an apprentice under him.

many charlatans, perhaps more than before, into the profession. As long as a patient has some money to pay, the *dibịa* has services to render - disease causing objects from the body to extract, sorcerous objects to expose, amulets to prepare etc. The question of competence ironically, is more easily neglected in the medical profession since the physician is never in short supply of explanations on why some development has occurred contrary to expectations. His infallibility is all the more enhanced when such explanations are based on the authority of some supernatural being, whom the *dibịa* alone has access to. Hence, the exploitation of the situations of sickness for personal financial gain becomes unlimited. In the past as it is today, no one controls the *dibịa* - his procedure, the diagnoses he makes and the medications he administers.

The leaders in many spiritual healing sects or Ministries which are found in all'corners and which claim to provide remedies to all ailments, perhaps better than the *dibịa,* appreciate the close relation between medicine and money. The principal mercenary motive of many of these sects is seen in their unlimited resourcefulness in dispossessing their clients of every money they have. In these healing homes, besides the official treatments and charges, the sick must buy specially blessed candles, soap, incense, creams, stickers, song cassettes etc. The high unemployment among the youth means that many more of them will answer the special call to be healing ministers in the ever-increasing healing homes.

Conclusion

Some opinions maintain that since Africans are increasingly making commitments to Christianity and modernity, studies into the nature and elements of African traditional religion would be serving mere academic interests. However, more than a superficial examination of the socio-religious phenomenon in Africa enables one to appreciate the continued vitality of the traditional religious world-view and the enormous influence it continues to wield in the lives of people. As it pertains to health and the traditional institutions that serve its cause, perceptions of disease causation which fashioned the traditional health institutions, are found to have received measures of legitimization by the similarities they have with Christian religious therapeutic views and modern medical holistic approach in defining health.

In most societies, the health institutions draw enthusiastic attention and remain very highly valued. Modern governments assign large proportions of the national annual budget to this sector. Traditional religious societies picked the most versatile and intelligent deities to superintend this area of human activity which is absolutely necessary for human happiness in the world. This deity inspired practitioners in the arduous work of disease diagnoses and endowed curers with cleverness of mind. Igbo society chose *agwụ* for this job. *Agwụ* is an appropriate choice because it is the spokesperson of the gods, and it is appointed by *Chukwu* to be the sharer and divider among the gods and certainly among men.

Human beings, it is believed, attain several perfections and pursue the realization of many other values through the patronage of *agwụ*. There exists the world-view endorsing the closeness of the supernatural and natural worlds which says, that the *dibịa's* world especially when he engages in the work of divination, is but a microcosm of the macro world of *agwu* and other spirits. A more precise assertion makes *agwu* dependent on the human reality for its manifestation and continued propagation or proliferation. The gap between transcendency and immanency becomes distorted. But these are assertions that paint a complex picture of reality and explain the apparent incomprehensibility of human conditions and fortunes. The use of the concept *agwu* to explain these, point to genuine human concern in Igbo religious history and hermeneutics.

Possession by which human beings find themselves under the influence of the spirits is a widely recognized phenomenon in most religions. The pre-initiatory and post-initiatory types of possession in relation to *agwu* demonstrate both the powers and the limitations of the deity. It does raise the question, why a deity would insist on bequeathing gifts on an unwilling human. *Agwu* who cudgels one into accepting its will may have little regard for the integrity of human mind and will. In this matter the case of *agwu* does raise questions for Igbo anthropology. But this phasic theory of possession ultimately enters into the many issues that pertain to the divine and the human. *Agwu* ambivalence and capriciousness are echoed therein. Human biophysical and psychological negative experiences as well as conditions of positive power and excellence are on the bases of the theory, rendered comprehensible within this socio-cultural area.

Our approach in this study was to see the indigenous religion and practices as the owners do and not to impose alien interpretations. In fidelity to this, this study relied very much on the local hermeneutical spirit. In that case, the researcher was very careful not to allow other religious backgrounds he might have to intrude into this, work.

The study has revealed the various sociological dimensions along which *agwu* is manifested. *Agwu* is a personal deity, but the person has dual sources of origin - agnate and enate. The person uses this deity to interact or to render services to other people. One eventually recognizes and remains in active relationship with other people who have like spirits. At the very end, the personal deity traces a path of what, from a socio-cultural perspective, is definition of person. The question of *agwu̧* ultimately is one of the fate of man in the world. Judaism, Christianity, ancient religions of Greece and Rome have sought to answer the question. *Agwu̧* is one of the answers Igbo religion has offered to explain good and evil, health and sickness and even life and death. It explains why the innocent suffers. Innocence is often deluding, for many who appear to be innocent carry the guilt of their past lives. These issues are at the very centre of *agwu̧* dogma. This dogma has the merit that for years it has provided answers to many questions in the society. However, today the claims of *agwu̧* must be examined in the light of those of other religions and of modern sciences.

The underlying conviction in this work is that the basic doctrine on which the traditional medical institutions have rested for centuries may have an important word to say to the present. This study is to make it possible that the word is clearly and distinctly uttered, not in the confused fashion of some Christian sect healers but in the critical way development of African ethnomedicine requires. It is a genuine argument that the eclectic practices in the ever-increasing numbers of Christian religious healing sects in present African societies could be prevented from growing more and more into practices of incongruous juxtapositions if the founders of these sects obtain sufficient knowledge of the indigenous world-view, beliefs, rites and practices. The optimism to guide studies of indigenous healing methods is based on the disposition which upholds that perspectives, methods, materials which originate from the indigenous institutions can be found useful and can be integrated into modern healing methods but such optimism must not overshadow the method of critical approach.

Appendix 1

Individual Experience Of *Agwʉ* Calling

Ali Nweke And The Strange Woman

In the interview granted by Ali Nweke, a *dibịa* (healer cum diviner) of Ogrute Ubo, Enugu-Ezike on 13th December, 1990, he narrated an account of his calling which I have given the title as above. His calling to this profession has a tinge of mystery about it. Ali's parents and the immediate ancestors of his lineage, were not diviners or healers. Traced through both his paternal and maternal lineages, there was no evidence of the *agwʉ* tradition. Ali in his childhood did not exhibit any of the early signs of calling and even if minor ones did exist, they could have passed unnoticed given the absence of 'expert eyes' in the family circle. Suddenly someday, the boy Ali was missing and did not reappear in the family until after four days. During this period, diviners soothed the anxiety of the parents by making them believe he was not lost forever, that he was not in any harm and had not been taken by slave dealers. They told the parents that Ali was on a type of journey. To the credit of these professionals, he came back the exact day they had predicted.

Within the period of his disappearance, an experience he compared to being in a dream, Ali was in the company of a strange woman who was teaching him the use of medicinal herbs and the art of healing. The first remedies she showed him were the antidote for snakebite as well as protection against witchcraft attacks. Up to the point of our meeting, Ali, who was about seventy years old had neither passed through any apprenticeship nor received any other form of professional training. All he knows and practices in healing and divination have been taught him by the spirits who after the first episode continued to appear to him in dreams. Other cures he was shown include those for infertility in women, impotency in men, insanity, convulsions, dysentery, and malaria.

Ali was equally taught the art of divination in dreams by another woman. This happened while he was still a boy. His knowledge of interpretation in divination baffled the experienced professionals. Faster and more accurately than seasoned diviners, he could decipher the fall of the *eha* (*afa*).

About such knowledge that had been granted to him by the sheer benevolence of the gods, Ali was instructed to observe certain ethical norms. He is never to commit murder by administering poisons nor to participate in conspiracy to murder or to hurt other people. In other words, the moral ethic of his work must commit him to the saving of life.

His welfare and that of his family, Ali is convinced, is the reason for the divine endowment. It gives him an occupation and a means of livelihood. This reason permeates his conception of his work and the actual practice of it. All he has learnt from the spirits are to be jealously guarded. He has not taught anyone the applications the gods have shown him. He believes that the spirits have the wisdom to choose whoever they wish to endow with whatever talent. In fact, he believes very strongly that the spirits would blame him and most likely withdraw the gift from him if he were not wise enough to preserve it exclusively for his use.

The strange woman who spirited Ali away in the first instance or the apparitions of the dreams are identified as *egere*. *Egere* is a female deity in the locality which is regarded as the patron of healers and diviners. Between *egere and agwu* several parallels exist. As with *agwu*, there are such names as *Nwaegere, Nwanyiegere. Egere* is recognized also as the inspirer of the sculptor, just as *agwu* is credited. Other deities in Enugu-Ezike such as *Akpuluocho, Adoro, Okeimufu* have personal *egere*. There are similarly *Agwuamadioha, Agwuala, Agwuimo* in other places. The symptoms of *egere* possession are identical with those of *agwu* possession. The fundamental characteristics of *agwu,* such as ambivalence and heredity are also found with *egere*. As there are paternal and maternal *agwu* so are there with *egere*. There is initiation into the cult of *egere* to establish the three fold functionaries - the priest, the physician and the diviner. The comparative survey makes it only too clear that the same spirit is called *agwu* and *egere* in the different localities.

There are minor disparities, however, in practices relating to *agwu* and *egere*. One is that there are no carved images of *egere*. The main symbol of the spirit is a bowl containing water which is placed at the back of the house, beside other spirit symbols or placed at the door of the house where the *dibia* does consultations.

Appendix 2

Obiora And The Symbolism Of *Akpu*

In the compound at Igbariam where Obiora Nwabude Madu lives, there stands a gigantic *akpu* tree (silk cotton), whose branches stretch extensively. The first impression a visitor to the place would have is the strange confidence which allows humans to live and move so close to it without fear of the hazardous threat the tree poses to human lives and habitation in the occasion of a storm. My visit to this compound was made in the company of Sr. Dr. Ebere Anosike and Father Godfrey Odigbo under the guidance of Mr. Sylvester Izualo, a native who had recommended Obiora as a great *dibia* in Igbariam. Immediately we arrived, the tree naturally caught our attention. None of us, except our guide, knew the deep symbolism of *akpu* in Igbo ritual. We were to learn later how the *akpu* provided for Obiora, the orientation to understand his calling as *dibia*, and the events in his life and that of his family.

Obiora, 48 years old, granted the interview on 12th June 1992. He was baptized a Catholic as a young person, like many of the other boys who attended Catholic schools. He did not, however, become a serious Christian as he admitted. He hardly attended Church services. When he wanted to marry he went in for a Christian marriage, not because he was convinced it was important, but to give the wife the chance to practice her faith as she wanted. The Church wedding was his last church attendance.

I shall present this case as much as possible in the sequence which the recorded interview followed. The accounts given by Obiora follow from the questions posed to him.

Early Indications of calling

As a boy Obiora was telepathic. He became inexplicably aware of certain events that happened in distant places. His father was always perturbed by the accuracy of his statements about such events. It made him to consult diviners about what might be happening to his boy. They always told him - *agwu no nwa gi n'ahu, o ga eme dibia (agwu*, is in your son's body, he will be *dibia*). In sleep Obiora claimed he was taken out by spirits. He made very little progress in school except in Mathematics where he excelled. He was, however, to drop from school ultimately. The disclosure of Obiora's

143

calling to be *dibia* was a great surprise to his father since the tradition was absent in his family as well as in the maternal lineage.

The Mysterious Akpu

At about the age of sixteen, Obiora discovered a young *akpu* plant springing up in their family compound. He pointed it out to his father and requested that the sapling should not be cut. Obiora had cause to leave the family for one month and on coming back discovered that his father had acted against his wish and had cut the sapling. He was deeply aggrieved but being a boy he did not know what line of action to take. Right from the moment he had found the plant some sympathetic virtue had swelled up in him towards it. He was all the more afflicted when his father was so unperceiving about his sentiments.

The night's dream justified his sympathetic attitude to the plant, for there it became most clear to him that the tree had great significance for him and his family. In this dream he had a vision whereby his brother was tied up. A hole was dug where the *akpu* had stood and he was dumped into it. The hole was not yet covered when Obiora woke up in fright. He narrated this dream to other members of the family.

Further Indications of Calling

The very same year the *akpu* was cut, Obiora's father fell seriously sick and soon died. He was appropriately buried. Obiora however, believed that his death was not unconnected with the *akpu*. Obiora himself fell victim of sorcerous attacks shortly. He showed us parts of his body with visible scars or even unhealed swellings. Maintenance of the family became part of his responsibility and he decided to be a farmer. In one year, he planted a field of rice which at first appeared most promising only later to suddenly change colour leading to very poor harvest. On consulting diviners he was told that the stump of the *akpu* plant which was cut was still alive and waited to be ritually appeased with sacrifices of kola nuts so that it could once more put up shoots. Then again he was instructed to acquire an *okuku* (a small gourd for storing medicine, to symbolize his readiness to embrace the *dibia* profession). Doing so offered the only check to impending troubles.

Reverse of Fortune

After Obiora had complied with the instructions of the diviner, the tiny shoot of the *akpu* reappeared. He built a hedge around it with sticks and warned the rest of the family against any further mistake. In the next planting season his rice harvest indicated a twist in fortune.

A Voice

At the end of the Nigeria/Biafra war, Obiora was poisoned by spirit agents who fired *mgbonsi* (disease causing objects) into his body. After consulting many medicine-men to no effect he decided to appeal to God. One day he sat down weeping and prayed to *Chukwu* (God):

O bu gi bu Chukwu kelu m
Ginwa weputara ahihia
Ginwa weputara mgborogwu
Si ya na ozizo di ya
Si ya na nke ogbugbu di ya
O bulu na oria gbue m
O bulu na ana afu gi bu Chukwu anya
Mu na gi kpee
Ife a akarika mu.

(You are God who created me
You provided leaves '.
You provided root
Made them to save
Made them to kill
If I die from this sickness
If it is possible to meet you, God
I will enter into judgement with you
This trouble has become too great for me.)

A few days after, Obiora heard a voice calling him but he saw no one. It instructed him to go into the forest with his knife and hoe. There in the forest some plants were pointed out to him and he obtained their roots. This was his first act as physician. As soon as Obiora drank a little of the decoction made from these roots the disease object that had been shot in his stomach through sorcerous attacks became most unquiet. After drinking more of it he discharged the poison which was in the form of a very dark object. This medication did not take care of the disease objects in his forehead and throat. The strange voice called him again on one bright afternoon and instructed him to apply the leaves of a certain shrub to his throat. After daily application for a week, a sore developed from which sticky substance was discharged. When he applied the medicine on his forehead a boil developed and when it was incised *mgbonsi* in the form of grains of sand were recovered. At the time of our visit Obiora's health problems had been solved except for some chronic ailment of his legs.

The Physician

Obiora's prominence as physician dramatically occurred. He applied a grass shown him by the strange voice to a sick man who had been given up as hopeless. He discovered the cause of the ailment was sorcery (*ndi uchichi gbara ya uta*). At the application of the medicine he was able to extract two pieces of foreign bone. This success won him outstanding fame in the town and other people with problems began to consult him.

Significance of Akpu

Obiora saw himself as a gift of God to the town of Igbariam. He is a gift brought about through reincarnation from his maternal lineage, symbolized by the *akpu* which is the very deity of this lineage. He described the *akpu* as *ihe mu siri puta uwa* (the channel of his reincarnation) and he sees the significance as *na mmadu putara uwa a si na onye o bu ji mgborogwu n'aka nri jide mgborogwu n'aka ekpe'*(that one enters the world holding medicinal roots in the right hand and in the left). *The akpu* therefore, is the source of his calling to the medical profession. This belief is implied as he asserts that *akpu* makes it possible for him to interact with *ndi mmuo* (spirits) and in his sleep hold discussions with the dead. The *akpu* is his guide who brings him to various corners of the spirit world.

Akpu has also great significance beyond the personal level. It had only three branches and according to Obiora, one branch represented him and the rest, his two brothers. This interpretation was confirmed for him when one of his brothers died and one of the branches of the *akpu* withered and fell off and for two years the tree stopped to grow. He pointed out to us the two remaining branches.

For his other brother the *akpu* has functioned as guide, urging him through dreams and visions to abandon evil ways and to respect and co-operate with him, now that he is the head of their family.

The Voice , Spirit, Akpu

Obiora believes that the voice he hears does not come in the form of inspiration but that it is actual voice. It comes always from behind. He turns but sees no one. In his town he is popularly called Obua but the voice addresses him as Obiora and he is able to know the difference.

Obiora traces the origin of the bangle he wears on the wrist to a group of six children he met in a trance. These children wore bangles. One of them had instructed him to acquire a similar bangle. This one had also addressed him as Obiora. These children, according to him, are spirits.

The bangle is called *ọnụigbo* and to wear it some taboos must be observed. Among them are: not to eat cassava, to avoid contact with a menstruating woman, and alcohol. The benefit is that whatever evil anyone discusses to the hearing of the bangle befalls the very speaker and designer of such evil.

A g w ụ, A kpụ

Akpụ is *agwụ* according to Obiora. *Akpụ*, which is the *arụsị* of his maternal home, has symbolism in the *akpụ* standing in his compound. It is this *arụsị* that had called him to be a *dibịa*. It is on account of this call that the tree had been given to him. It also endows other people with special talents such as trading or teaching. Yet his actual initiation as *dibịa* required the installation of *arọbunagụ*. This is a symbol of *agwụ* which a *dibịa* inherits from the maternal uncles at his initiation.

The spirit *akpụ* is female. That is Obiora's experience in dreams. Before he married, this spirit used to visit him frequently. At the end of the visit he always escorted her to a particular point on the pathway and she would vanish.

About *agwụ*, he explains that when it possesses a woman it adopts female qualities (*o wele mmụọ nke nwanyị sowe nwanyị*) and in the case of a man it embraces male characteristics. Hence, the taboos a woman observes for her *agwụ* are different from those that the man observes.

Initiation

This is called *emume agwụ or emume arọbunagụ or ịrụ agwụ*. It is the rite for the installation of the spirit, *agwụ*. The officiants at this ceremony are usually from the maternal home - *ndị ikwunne*. There is the official giving of *okuku* to the initiate and the erecting of a shrine. This shrine consists of two clay pots buried upside down and the planting of *ogirisi*. Sacrifices of fowls and kola are made. Yams and fish are provided for preparing the flesh of the victims for a feast. The maternal relations who have brought along their *okwukwu agwụ* must make sure it is sent back home before the fall of da   ss. The actual celebration of the initiation takes place three weeks latei. At the feast known as *otite*, friends and relatives are invited.

Festival of *A g w ụ*

In Igbariam, the festival period for *agwụ* is the seventh month. Depending on one's financial standing, sacrifice of fowl or goat is offered by those who have *agwụ*. After the flesh has been cooked, part of the food is presented and

offered to the spirit. Below is a sample of the accompanying prayer that
Obiora says at the occasion:

Chukwu ọ bụ gị nyelụ m ọlụ a mụ na-alụ
Mụ adụrụrụ ya nụbụ
Ọz izọ ka m biara, mụ abiaghị ogbugbu
Mụ na-agọ ọfọ nwoke, na-agọ ọfọ nwanyị
Mụ si nwoke dịrị, nwanyị dịrị
N'obodo Igbariam mụ biara, mmepe ka m n'ekwu
Ihe dị mma biawa na Igbariam

Akpụ-enyi m!
Chukwu ọ bụ gị nyere m akpụ-enyi
Ọz izọ ka mụ dị, mụ adịg hị n'ogbugbu.
Olili ka mụ chọlụ ka mụ nye gị taa
Na mụ na-enye gị bụ ka mụ nye chaa gị,
Ka ahụ dị mụ bụ Obiora mma,
Dị nwanyị mụ mma,
Dị ezi n'ụlọ mụ mma,
Dị kwasị obodo anyị bụ Igbariam mma.
Nalụ nụ lie.
Ọ bụlụ na mụ welụ aka nwata nye ụnụ
Ụnụ welụ aka okenye nara m.

Arọbunagụ! Agwụ nwe m!
Ọ bụlụ na mụ welụ ọnụ nwatakịlị wee na-akpọ ụnụ
Welụ nụ ọnụ ruo welu na na m
Na m bụ kwanị nwata
Ọkụ e nyelụ nwatakịlị adị arụ ya arụ.
Egbe belụ ugo belụ
nke si ibe ya ebele
ya gosị ebe ọ ga-ebe.
Nri, nrie ọfụma
otite gị ka anyị na efe
Ka anyị rie nri, ka anyị rite ife ọma.

(Chukwu it is you who gave me this work which I do
I did not snatch it by force
I am to save, not to destroy
I wish that it goes well with man and woman
I pray that man lives and woman lives
I have come to this town Igbariam to speak of development
May what is good come to Igbariam.

Akpụ my friend
Chukwu it is you who gave me *akpụ* my friend
I am to save people not to destroy them.
Today I have come to offer you food.
I give you in order to win from you good health for me, Obiora,
Good health for my wife
Good health for members of my family
And good health for my town Igbariam.
Accept and eat
If I present my offering with the hands of a child,
Accept it with the hands of an elder.

Arọbunagụ! Agwụ to whom I belong!
If I invoke you in the child's voice
Reach out and hear me
For I am but a child
Fire given to a child does not hurt him
Let the kite perch and let the eagle perch
If one says no to the other
Let him point out to him where to perch
This is food, eat well
It is your glory I worship
As we eat, may what is good be ours.

Glossary of Igbo Words and Expressions

Abọ/avọ agwụ	The ritual basket where agwụ icons are stored. Every medicine-man owns such a basket and it is revered as sacred because of its contents.
Abọsị	A popular ritual plant in Igboland.
Adoro	Deity of Enugu-Ezike, a northern Igbo town.
Afa	The Igbo form of divinatory system.
Agbara/ Arụsi(alụsi)	Generic name for deities.
Ahiajọku/ Ahianjọku/ Ihinjọku	The yam spirit-force; an annual festival exists in its honour.
Ajọ mmụọ	Evil spirit.
Aka-ikpa agwụ	The left hand of agwụ which symbolizes attributes of ambivalence, capriciousness and deceitfulness.
Aka-nri agwụ	The right hand of agwụ which symbolizes positive attributes
Akaraka/akalaka	Destiny or natural gift.
Akparata	Name of afa in Enugu-Ezike, a northern Igbo town.
Akpụ	Silk cotton, can be sign of vocation from agwụ.
Akpụlọcha	Deity of Enugu-Ezike.
Ala/Ana/Anị	The physical earth; the earth goddess who is the custodian of morality.
Amadiọha	God of thunder and lightning.
Anya afa	Diviners eyes (lit.); medicinal preparation administered into the eyes that enables one to 'see' as a diviner. It helps the development of potentials for becoming a diviner.
Anya mbelelu agwụ	Symbol of agwụ constant watchfulness.
Anya nsi	Medicinal preparation to enable one develop the keen eyes of a physician.
Anyanwụ	The sun/sun god.
Chukwu/Chineke/ Chukwuabịama	The supreme deity of Igbo religion.
Ebubeagụ	A plant specie found often at the shrines.
Echuchuu	A plant found often at the shrines.
Egere	Deity of Enugu-Ezike with characteristics similar to those of agwụ.

Eke, Orie, Afọ, Nkwọ	Igbo four-day week.
Ekike	Amulet.
Ekwele m agwụ	I say yes to *agwụ;* ritual of consent in *agwụ* initiation.
Ekwum agwụ	The core symbols of the *ulọ agwụ*
Epha	Urhobo system of divination which is similar to *afa.*
Ifa	Yoruba system of divination which is similar to *afa.*
Igwe	The sky/sky god.
Ikenga	Spirit force of achievement, represented sometimes with the up-thrusting horns of the ram.
Itụ anya	Rite of initiation to open the eyes.
Kamalụ	God of thunder and lightning.
Mbe	Tortoise, used in rite of initiation and in divination.
Mgbọnsi	Disease objects which are intruded into the body of the victim.
Nkịta anya anọ	Dog with shedding on the upper eyebrows particularly valued for rituals.
Nkuku ọgwụ	Gourd used to store powdered medicine.
Nwa egere	Name given in acknowledgement of the influence of *egere* at the birth of a child.
Nwanyị egere	Name given to a female child in acknowledgement of the influence of *egere* at her birth.
Nzu	White chalk used for various rituals and for decoration.
Ọbasị	Another name for Supreme God.
Obi evule	A ram's heart which is used in the rite of *dibịa* initiation.
Odo	A secret cult society found in northern parts of Igboland. It has a lot of social and religious influence in the society.
Odu	Yoruba divinatory recitation.
Ọfọ	Symbol object of authority and justice possessed by heads of families, priests of deities, diviners and physicians.
Ọgbanje	Evil spirits which reincarnate repeatedly in children.
Ọgbedega	Another name for *afa* in Enugu-Ezike, a northern Igbo town.
Ogirisi	(Newbouldia Laevis), a very popular Igbo ritual plant.
Ogu	Symbol of innocence and moral uprightness. It works closely with *ọfọ.*

Ọgwu	A generic term that can indicate medicines, poisons, protective preparations, magical acts.
Ọha	(Pterocarpus Soyauxii), a ritual plant, the leaves are popular vegetables.
Ọjị	Iroko tree which sometimes is sign of vocation from *agwu*
Okeimufu	A deity of Enugu-Ezike.
Ọkọnkọ	A secret society that flourishes in parts of southern Igboland.
Ọkpuebo	The carver ; *ebo* was the popular wood for carving in Mbaise area.
Okwe	Lima bean (Phaseolus Lanatus), used as *afa* beads.
Okwukwu agwu	Name for main *agwu* symbol inside *ulo agwu*.
Ọmụ (Nkwụ)	A tendril of the palm tree used to mark out a tabooed object, area or person.
Ose ọjị	(Aframonum Malegueta), spicy seed which is eaten together with kola nut and it is also used widely in rituals.
Ọzọ	The prestigious title of the Igbo people, for males only.
Ụda	African or Guinea pepper (Xylopia Aethiopicum), a tree that produces spicy fruits used in *dibịa* initiation.
Ụdara	Star apple (Chrysophylum Excelsa) grows to a big size. The roots are used to make symbol objects of *agwu*.
Udele	The vulture, used in the symbolic codification of *agwu* attribute of keen perception.
Ugiri agbọlọ	Native mango used to make *afa* beads.
Ulili	The squirrel, symbol of *agwu* prevision and foresightedness.
Ụlọ agwu	The *dibịa's* office where he consults with clients and where his cult paraphernalia are stored.
Ụrụala agwu	Symbol of *agwu* attributes of ambivalence, capriciousness and deceitfulness.

List of Informants

Name	Age	Place	Status/Occupation	Date of Interview
Abugu Onu Onoja	ca.85	Mkpante Ulo Enugu Ezike	Diviner cum physician	13/12/90
Abumbu	ca. 73	Amaekwu Lokpanta	Diviner	20/11/94
Afike Nwankwo	ca. 65	Ubaha Nnaka	Agwu devotee	24/6/92
Akunne	ca. 50	Nri	Museum attendant	29/8/92
Alaribe Nzeji	ca. 85	Ezuhu Nguru Mbaise	Elder and traditional religious leader	26/6/92
Ama John Chima (Chief Dr.)	ca. 72	Ekoli Edda	Diviner cum Physician	5/8/93
Anyanwu Oparaku(Chief/Eze Dibia)	ca.65	Ekwereazu Mbaise	Diviner cum Physician	17/2/91 (also 10/3/92)
Anyanwu Patrick	38	Umuokirika Ekwereazu	Diviner cum Physician	21/7/92
Azonuche Otekenubia	ca. 60	Illah	Diviner cum Physician	15/3/92
Edoko Agbaedo	ca. 60	Ikpamodo Enugu-Ezike	Diviner	12/12/90
Eze Fidelis	ca 56	Ikpamodo Enugu-Ezike	Diviner cum Physician	12/12/90
Kalu Aja	ca. 75	Atani Arochukwu	Diviner cum Physician	10/6/91
Kalu Okoro	ca.60	Ihechiowa	Diviner cum healer	19/9/91
Ikenwe P. N.	ca 56	Illah, Delta State	Catechist	19/8/91
Ikenwe Christiana	ca. 40	Illah, Delta State	House wife	19/8/91
Madugba Nwogu (Chief)	ca. 75	Ama-asa Obioma Ngwa	Diviner cum Physician,(holder of title omeudo 1 of Ama-asa)	29/3/91
Madu Nwabude Obiora	ca. 48	Igbariam	Diviner and Physician	12/5/92
Maduka Ibara	ca. 65	Uturu	Retired civil servant, Farmer, Community head	12/3/92

153

Njoku Uzosike	ca.58	Ezuhu Nguru Mbaise	*Agwu* cult leader	6/5/89.
Nwankwo Aforibe	ca.38	Nkoto Ihube Okigwe	Diviner	5/10/90
Nweke Ali	ca.70	Ogrute Ulo Enugu-Ezike	Diviner cum Physician	13/12/90
Nwiga Ali	ca. 80	Mkpante, Enugu-Ezike	Diviner cum Physician	13/12/90
Nwatamole	ca.75	Umuonye-aliagwo Mbieri	Diviner cum Physician (healer of water spirit possession)	15/3/92
Nwokocha Uchegulem	ca.60	Nkoto Ihube	Diviner cum Physician	2/8/91
Okali Onyiro Basil	ca.78	Umuka Okigwe	Community elder and religious leader	6/6/90
Okeoma Mishark Uhuohuo	ca. 78	Umuogo Achara Uturu	Diviner cum Physician	17/6/89
Okonkwo Ambrose	ca. 65	Nri	Retired civil servant	24/8/92
Okonkwo Okereke	ca. 90	Nri	Elder, Religious head and *agwu* devotee	24/8/92
Okonu Agwu	ca.56	Ekoli Edda	Farmer,and Physician	5/8/93
Olo John Ama (Chief)	ca.73	Amato Obioma Ngwa	Diviner cum Physician	29/3/91
Onwuka Obinali	ca.80	Akokwa	Diviner cum Physician	4/2/91
Onyeakobusi Uwakwe	ca.75	Nkoto Ihube	*Ozo* title holder and ritual head of the community	5/10/90
Osuichie Okorie	ca. 70	Amamiri Ihechiowa	Farmer, traditional religious leader	28/10/89
Ubi Nweni	ca.75	Ekpo Ihechiowa	Farmer, traditional religionist	25/6/89
Ukwuaba Edoko	ca.70	Ikpamodo, Enugu-Ezike		13/12/90
Uwanekwuka Anthony	ca. 59	Mkplogwu Ogboegene, Illah	Diviner	19/8/91

Participants At The Group Interview At Ekoli Ludu.

All the participants are kindred heads ana are above 50 years old. Some are over 70 years. The head of this group is Chief Anuma Ugbo who is also the head of the traditional religion of Edda and mostly all in the group are traditional religionists. The interview took place on 5/8/93.

Anuma Ugbo (Eze Egbela 1 of Edda)
Arua Ibiam
Arunsi Ndukwe
Chima Ndukwe (Chief)
Chima Nkama
Effa Emmanuel
Ejem Oji Ama (Chief)
Ibiam Nkama
Irem Nkama
Igwe Oji Ama
Okoro Ama
Onu Irem Ibiam
Ude Kara Uduma
Uro Agwu Agba
Uduma Nkama

Bibliography

Books

Achebe, Chinua, *Things Fall Apart,* London: Heinemann, 1958.
_____*Arrow of God* London: Heinemann 1964.
Achebe, Chinwe, *The World of the Ogbanje,* Enugu: Fourth Dimension, 1986.
Aligwekwe, P.E., *The Continuity of Traditional Values in the African Society: the Igbo of Nigeria,* Abuja: Totan Publishers, 1991.
Anosike, Eberechukwu M., *A Modern Healer: The life and Work of Dr. Cyril Ekenwa O. Nwogu,* Uturu (Nigeria): Imo State University Press, 1992.
Arnulf, Camps, *Partners in Dialogue,* New York: Orbis Books, 1983.
Arinze, Francis A., *Sacrifice in Ibo Religion,* Ibadan: Ibadan University Press, 1970.
Awolalu, Omosade J. & P. Adelumo Dopamu, *West African Traditional Religion,* Ibadan: Onibonoje Press, 1974.
Bascom, William R. & J. Milville Herskovits (eds), *Continuity and Change in African Cultures,* Chicago: The University of Chicago Press, 1965.
Basden, G.T., *Niger Ibos,* London: Frank Cass & Co. 1966.
_____*Among the Ibos of Nigeria,* Lagos: University Publishing Edition, 1982.
Beattie, John, *Other Cultures,* London: Routledge & Kegan Paul, 1964.
Douglas, Mary, *Purity and Danger: An Analysis of Concepts of Pollution and Taboo,* London: Routledge & Kegan Paul, 1966.
Echeruo, Michael J.C., "A Matter of Identity" (1979 Ahiajoku Lecture), Owerri: Culture Division, Ministry of Information, Culture, Youth & Sports, 1979.
Eke, Peter P. & Ashiwaju Garba (eds.), *Nigeria Since Independence: The first 25 years,* Ibadan: Heinemann Educational Books, 1989.
Ekechi, F.K., *Missionary Enterprise and Rivalry in Igboland 1857 - 1914,* London: Frank Cass & Co., 1972.
Eliade, Mircea, *Symbolism, the Sacred, the Art,* New York: Crossroad, 1986.
Ezekwugo, Christopher U.M., *Chi: the true God in Igbo Religion,* Alwaye, Kerele India: Pontifical Institute of Philosophy and Theology, 1987.

Gennep, Van A., *The Rites of Passage*, London: Routledge and Kegan Paul, 1977.

Hastings, Adrian, *African Christianity*, London: Geoffrey Chapman, 1976.

Henderson, Richard N., *The King in Every Man*, New Haven: Yale University Press, 1972.

Hiebert, Paul G., *Cultural Anthropology*, Philadelphia: J.B. Lippincott, 1979.

Ibe Elias Dike *Igbo Customs and Traditions*, Lagos: Diceson Associates, 1989.

Idowu, E.B., *African Traditional Religion: A Definition*, London: SCM Press, 1973.

Ifeanyi, Victor, *The Catholic Church and the Challenges of Traditional System of Health Care in Nigeria*, Rome, 1986.

Ikenga-Metuh, Emefie, *God and Man in African Religion*, London: Geoffery Chapman, 1981.

_____*African Religions in Western Conceptual Schemes: The Problem of Interpretation*, Bodija Ibadan: Pastoral Institute, 1985.

_____(ed.) *The Gods in Retreat: Continuity and Change in African Religion*, Enugu: Fourth Dimension Publishers, 1986.

_____*Comparative Studies of African Traditional Religion*, Onitsha (Nigeria): IMICO Publishers, 1987.

Ilogu, Edmund, *Christianity and Igbo Culture*, London: NOK Publishers, 1976.

Jordan, John P., *Bishop Shanahan of Southern Nigeria*, Dublin: Conmore & Reynolds, 1948.

Leith-Ross, Sylvia, *African Woman*, London: Routledge and Kegan Paul, 1965 (first published in 1939).

Malefijt, Annemarie de Waal, *Religion and Culture: An Introduction to Anthropology of Religion*, New York: Macmillan, 1968.

Mbiti, John, *Introduction to African Religion*, London: Heinemann, 1975.

Nnadozie, Josef Awazie, "Offspring *(Ọmụmụ)* in Nguru Traditional Marriage", Thesis presented for B.D., Bigard Memorial Seminary, Enugu, 1978.

Nwoga, Donatus I., "*Nka na Nzere*: The Focus of Igbo World-view" (1984 Ahiajoku Lecture), Owerri: Culture Division, Ministry of Information, Culture, Youth and Sports, 1984.

_____*The Supreme God as Stranger in Igbo Religious Thought*, Ekwereazu (Imo State): Hawk Press, 1984.

Odoemene, Anacletus Nnamdi, *The Challenges of Igbo Identity*, München: Hochshule für Philosophie, 1983.

Okigbo B.N., "Plants and Food in Igbo Culture" (1980 Ahiajoku Lecture, Owerri: Culture Division, Ministry of Information, Culture, Youth · and Sports, 1980.

Onwuejeogwu, M.A., *An Igbo Civilization: Nri Kingdom and Hegemony*, London: Ethiope Publishing Corporation, 1981.

Orji, J. H., "Agwu among the Ikeduru of Mbaitoli/Ikeduru Local Government Area"(An unpublished Thesis presented for a B.A. at the University of Nigeria, Nsukka, 1979).

Otto, Rudolf, *The Idea of the Holy*, London: Oxford University Press, 1923.

Quarcoopome, T.N.O., *West African Traditional Religion*, Ibadan: African University Press, 1987.

Ray, B.C., *African Religions: Symbol, Ritual and Community*, New Jersey: Prentice-Hall, 1976.

Sanneh, L., *West African Christianity: Religious Impact*, New York: Orbis Books, 1983.

Schillebeeckx, Edward, *Christ: The Christian Experience in the Modern, World*, London, SCM Press, 1982.

Skorupski, John, *Symbols and Theory*, Cambridge: Cambridge University Press, 1976.

Talbot, Amaury, *The Peoples of Southern Nigeria*, London: Frank Cass & Co., 1969.

Thomas, Northcote W., *Law and Custom of the Ibo of Awka Neighbourhood S. Nigeria*, London: Harrison and Sons, 1913.

Wach, Joachim, *Sociology of Religion*, Chicago: The University of Chicago Press, 1971 (first published 1944).

Zahan, Dominic, *The Religion, Spirituality, and Theory of Traditional Africa*, Chicago: University of Chicago Press, 1970.

Articles

Acholonu Catherine O. "Folklore Origins of the Igbo," *Nigeria Magazine*, vol. 55, No 4, Oct-Dec., 1987.

Afigbo, A.E., "Traditions of Igbo Origin: A Comment." *Nigeria Magazine*, No. 144, 1983.

Aguwa, Jude C. U., "Taboos and Purification of Ritual Pollutions in Igbo Traditional Society: Analysis and Symbolisms." *Anthropos* 88(1993).

Amara, B.I., "Possession - Its Nature and Modes." *The Sierra Leone Bulletin of Religion*, Vol.6, No.2, December, 1964.

Christensen, James Boyd, "The Adaptive Functions of Fanti Priesthood." In William R. Bascom and Milville J. Herskovits, (eds.), *Continuity and Change in African Cultures*, Chicago: The University of Chicago Press, 1965.

Ejizu, C.I., "The Taxonomy, Provernance and Functions of *Ọfọ*, A Dominant Igbo Ritual and Political Symbol. *Anthropos* 82(1987).

_____ *Ritual enactment of Achievement: Ikenga Symbol in Igboland*, PAIDEUMA 37 (1991)

Foster, G.N.; "An Introduction to Ethnomedicine." In R. H. Bannerman, J. Burton, W.C. Wen, (eds) *Traditional Medicine and Health Care Coverage*, Geneva: WHO, 1983.

Ikobi, Goddy, "Healing and Exorcism: The Nigerian Pastoral Experience." In Chris U. Manus., Luke N. Mbefo & E. E. Uzukwu (eds), *Healing and Exorcism: The Nigerian Experience*, Attakwu (Enugu): Spiritan International School of Theology, 1992.

Kalu, Ogbu C., "Religion and Social Control in Igboland". In Jacob K. Olupoma, &Sulayman S. Nyang, (eds.), *Religious Plurality in Africa: Essays in Honour of John S. Mbiti*, Berlin: Mouton de Gruyter, 1993.

Nabofa, M.Y. & Ben Elegbuo, "Epha: Urhobo System of Divination and its Esoteric Language." *Orita: Ibadan Journal of Religious Studies* (XXX/1, June 1981).

Onaiyekan, John, "The Priesthood in Owe Traditional Religion." In Adegbola, E.A.,(ed.) *Traditional Religion in West Africa*, Ibadan: Daystar Press, 1983.

Tillich, Paul, "Culture as Expression of Ultimate Concern." In Edward Cell (ed.), *Religion and Contemporary Western Culture*, New York: Nashville Abingdon,1967.

Turner, Victor, "Betwixt and Between: The Liminal Period in Rites de Passage". In Lessa William A. & Evon Z. Vogt (eds.) *Readers in Comparative Religion*, 4th ed., New York: Harper & Row , 1979.

Index

160

www.ingramcontent.com/pod-product-compliance
Lightning Source LLC
Chambersburg PA
CBHW021829020426
42334CB00014B/542